Deconstructing
Early Childhood Education

Rethinking Childhood

Joe L. Kincheloe and Janice A. Jipson
General Editors

Vol. 2

PETER LANG
New York • Washington, D.C./Baltimore • Boston
Bern • Frankfurt am Main • Berlin • Vienna • Paris

Gaile Sloan Cannella

Deconstructing
Early Childhood Education

Social Justice and Revolution

PETER LANG
New York • Washington, D.C./Baltimore • Boston
Bern • Frankfurt am Main • Berlin • Vienna • Paris

Library of Congress Cataloging-in-Publication Data

Cannella, Gaile Sloan.
Deconstructing early childhood education: social justice and revolution /
Gaile Sloan Cannella.
p. cm. — (Rethinking childhood; v. 2)
Includes bibliographical references and index.
1. Early childhood education—Social aspects. 2. Postmodernism and
education. 3. Critical pedagogy. 4. Child development. I. Title. II. Series.
LB1139.23.C36   372.21—dc20   96-19870
ISBN 978-0-8204-3452-0
ISSN 1086-7155

Die Deutsche Bibliothek-CIP-Einheitsaufnahme

Cannella, Gaile Sloan:
Deconstructing early childhood education: social justice and revolution /
Gaile Sloan Cannella. –New York, Washington, D.C./Baltimore; Boston; Bern;
Frankfurt am Main; Berlin; Vienna; Paris: Lang.
(Rethinking childhood; Vol. 2)
ISBN 978-0-8204-3452-0
NE: GT

Cover design by James F. Brisson.

The paper in this book meets the guidelines for permanence and durability
of the Committee on Production Guidelines for Book Longevity
of the Council of Library Resources.

© 1997, 2002, 2005, 2008 Peter Lang Publishing, Inc., New York
29 Broadway, 18th Floor, New York, NY 10006
www.peterlang.com

Printed in the United States of America.

Contents

Introduction
Joe L. Kincheloe, Series Editor

Gaile Cannella is not intimidated by the shibboleths of early childhood education. The point here is to examine the taken–for–granted assumptions of the field in a manner that exposes modern science's regulatory impulse and tendency for universalization. Concerned with the internal contradictions of a field that promotes fulfillment and happiness for all children, Cannella astutely deconstructs the unquestioned values, standards, and meanings that limit children's options. The scientific globalization of childhood promoted by mainstream developmental psychology has not served the interests of children from non–white and poor backgrounds. When specific students fail to meet the mileposts of developmentalism, they are deemed the ones in need of adjustment; the cultural appropriateness of the mileposts themselves are often left unquestioned. In a style that is theoretically informed but crisp in its clarity, Cannella carefully analyzes these points and more in her attempt to restructure the twentieth century conversation about young children and their education.

Deconstructing Early Childhood Education: Social Justice and Revolution represents an important moment in the larger revolution of childhood studies. Along with a cadre of other pioneers, Cannella refuses to accept traditional notions of child development, the sacrosanct research methods used to study childhood, the portrayal of childhood as a fixed, unchanging entity, or the "validated" educational strategies used to teach young children. At the same time she understands these dynamics; Gaile appreciates the fact that those who advocate the traditional view are typically individuals who have dedicated their lives to making life better for children. As she points out in Chapter 8 of this work, her attempt is not to simply debase the work of childhood educators who came before her. Her effort is to catalyze a critical conversation about the discourse of early childhood in a way that opens to view perspectives that are too often oppressive in their efforts.

In this context, it is easy to appreciate Cannella's contribution to a critical constructivist literature. Understanding that the backgrounds and cultural expectations of all observers, scholars in particular, inform their perceptions, she asserts that social, cultural, and political factors influence this complex, constructivist process. Indeed, cultural signs, linguistic codes, unexamined epistemologies, and embedded power play an exaggerated role in shaping assumptions about ourselves and our social worlds. As a critical in shaping assumptions about ourselves and our social worlds. As a critical constructivist Cannella is interested in these power dynamics, in the way discourses and ideologies influence our constructions of the world. When questions of power are pursued in the context of childhood studies, interesting things happen. Child development comes to be viewed as an imperialistic notion that positions particular social groups as backward and others as advanced. The superiority of one form of childhood is used as a means of delegitimating other forms. Even the role of women in this discourse is severely limited, for within the patriarchal discipline of early childhood education women are expected to be nurturing caregivers and babysitters. Such a gender dynamic has often undermined efforts to establish early childhood practice as a scholarly theoretically informed activity. One of the most important parts of this book involves Cannella's compelling vision of "what could be" in a reconceptualized early childhood field, what it might mean to escape the multiple boundaries of the truncated discipline.

Refusing the seduction of specified blueprints for reinvented early childhood studies, the author allows for multiple responses to her deconstructive project. Her value–laden pedagogical and psychological imagination is dedicated both to critical cultural work and to a continual critique of the explicitly held values that ground it. Rejecting the modernist view of the psychologized child, Cannella's reconceptualized practitioner watches for middle class mimesis — the establishment of middle class values and ways of seeing as a barometer by which everyone is evaluated. As a handbook for early childhood educators dedicated to escaping the webs of power the discipline has successfully spun, *Deconstructing Early Childhood Education* will occupy a central role in the revolution of childhood studies. As co-editor of the *Rethinking Childhood* series at *Peter Lang*, I am honored to have played a bit part in the publication of this exemplary, groundbreaking, and highly readable book.

Preface and Acknowledgments

This book represents a pathway in a long journey, a personal journey that began with a concern for the group of people that we have categorized as "children." The book is not designed to provide "right" answers, but to question the very existence of a predetermined "rightness" imposed by one group on another. The purpose is to further the critical dialogue begun in early childhood education by such scholars as Bloch, Kessler, Lubeck, Silin, and Tobin and to introduce notions of reconceptualization as proposed by Apple, Pinar, Grumet, and others. My desire is that diverse readers will engage in multiple forms of critique, examining even those assumptions about childhood and education that have been so thoroughly accepted as truth that they are not questioned.

The message of any book is limited in a variety of ways by the boundaries of language, the languages that others have constructed for us and the language that binds our personal ways of communicating with and in the world. In this work, I use the language of others both to focus on cultural ways of thinking and to demonstrate our limits. As examples, in particular sections, I refer to all people as "man" to illustrate the enlightenment and modernist focus on male dominance. The term "Third World" is used, illustrating the modernist and imperialist notion that particular peoples and countries are inferior to others. The term "child" is used, a label that those who are older have placed on a particular group that they would "protect." I hope that as the reader completes the text, language itself will be called into question, will be considered and examined as a social, political, power–laden force that privileges some and oppresses others.

Throughout the book, I use language to refer to my own personal perspectives by using the word "I" and in reference to my connections with other early childhood educators, parents, women, and adults by using the terms "we" and "our." I recognize (and accept as legitimate) that some readers will not be comfortable with my use of "we" and "our." I would simply ask that the terms be understood as representing the connections and experiences that some of us, perhaps with similar cultural, educational, and political backgrounds, share. The terms and the ideas associated with them are not presented as universally applicable, but as words for demonstrating potentially common bonds.

Acknowledgment is meant to honor those who have influenced and cared for us, those who have impacted our knowing and supported us in our everyday lives. I honor those who have influenced me through their scholarly work: Erica Burman, bell hooks, Valerie Walkerdine, Joe Kincheloe, Shirley Steinberg, Yvonna Lincoln, John Stansell, Rafael Lara-Alecio. Further, I acknowledge the following with affection and gratitude: My husband, Bert, my children, Christina and Steven, and my parents, Donald and Helen Sloan. Finally, I honor and dedicate this book to all those people, both young and old, that we have not heard, people whose voices have been silenced by our predetermined expectations about and for them. May we learn to respect, hear, and appreciate each other.

Chapter I

Why Critique the Field?

We must learn to be vulnerable enough to allow our world to turn upside down in order to allow the realities of others to edge themselves into our consciousness.

Delpit, 1993, p. 139

As Euro–American early childhood educators, we consider ourselves advocates for children. We take pride in the notion that we are child–centered and place the whole child at the forefront of our thoughts and actions. Through observation and psychological theory, we have diligently learned so much about children that we can describe how they grow and change. We know what kind of experiences to provide for them and how to advise others regarding these experiences. We dedicate many hours to issues of child development, attempting to improve home and school experiences for all children.

Yet, have our efforts actually led to increased acceptance and opportunity for all children? Have our efforts resulted in younger members of society who are treated as human beings rather than as property? Human beings (including children) live with violence on the streets of their neighborhoods. Increasingly larger numbers of them from particular groups live in poverty. As mortal creatures, children and adults alike deal with illness and death on a regular basis. The communication and socioeconomic gaps (including access to resources) between human beings from different cultural groups and economic classes is widening in the United States and around the world. Monied children attend particular schools while poor children are provided with different experiences. Even in preschool classrooms, gendered power is exhibited by young males. We could go on and on and on.

Obviously, we cannot entirely change the world, or even a particular society, by successfully using any one teaching method with all children, however child–centered and developmentally appropriate the technique is judged to be. Societal issues are much too complex. But what of the school world; are we creating early childhood education in which social injustices and inequities are diminished? Some early childhood educators (Cannella, in press; Kessler, 1991; Silin, 1987) have proposed that the knowledge base used to ground the field actually serves to support the status quo, reinforces prejudices and stereotypes, and ignores the real lives of children (and other human beings such as their parents and teachers). Without analyzing the assumptions with which we function, we may actually be contributing to the inequities and social injustices that many experience in our society. Unless we problematize (Foucault, 1980) the beliefs and practices that have guided the field of early childhood education to uncover hidden histories, biases, and illusions, we risk supporting a restrictive and narrow perspective. We risk excluding human beings whose lives do not mirror our dominant view of early childhood; and we place limits on ourselves and the children with whom we interact.

The purpose of this book is to deconstruct early childhood education, identifying and evaluating the themes and forms of discourse that have dominated the field, leading to the construction of specific theories and forms of practice (Burman, 1994, Derrida, 1981). The goal of deconstruction is to reveal inconsistencies, contradictions, and biases within those dominating themes.

The first theme is the construction of "childhood" as a form of existence that is separate and distinct from "adulthood." This concept of childhood is examined by conducting a genealogy of childhood (Chapter 2), analyzing the hidden assumptions underlying the official child development text (Chapter 3), and identifying the dominant themes that privilege early experience as the determiner of life (Chapter 4). The second theme, the construction of the field of early childhood education, is explored, problematizing our stories of institutionalized early education and care (Chapter 5), examining child–centered, play–based perspectives (Chapter 6), and exploring the professionalization of early childhood education (and education in general) as an instrument for the regulation of women and children (Chapter 7).

Finally, I agree with the notion that "deconstruction without reconstruction is an act of irresponsibility" (Putnam, quoted by Appleby, 1994, p. 234). No decisions would be made, no actions taken, if we simply deconstruct. For this reason, an alternative avenue for early childhood education is posited in Chapter 8, Early Education as the Struggle for Social Justice. This perspective is not mine originally (See Bloch, 1987; Kessler & Swadener, 1992; Pinar, 1975, 1994) and should not be viewed as the "correct" focus for the field, but one possibility among many. Just as we would hope our children would not be dominated by one view of the world, perhaps we should establish that same goal for our professional field.

My Biases

Before deconstructing the themes that have dominated the field, I feel that I must explain my own philosophical perspective. As with most of us in early childhood education, my views have been influenced by the Euro–American dominant historical knowledge base, the history that we "know." This history and the knowledge constructed within it has grounded our beliefs about children, our decisions for them, and our actual practice. For most of us, the knowledge provided by our common historical perspective is so embedded within ourselves and our own culture (e.g. white, patriarchal, middle-class, Euro–American, educated) that we have not conceptualized the need to question the history/knowledge that we "know."

Secondly, I have come to believe that our knowledge of children and what is best for them has resulted in the silencing of human voices that are not ours. Voices of "silent knowing" are those of the actual children with whom we work as they live their real lives in settings that we have not comprehended, as they display strengths and understandings that we have not dreamed of, and as they construct knowledges that would challenge the boundaries of our own worlds. These voices of "silent knowing" are also those of parents and community members whose life experiences represent different cultural strengths than our own, whose interactions with children represent rich histories that we have not experienced. These voices are living their everyday lives in our societies and our world right now in poverty, in affluence, with prejudice, with privilege, with limitations, and with opportunity.

Further, as a population of mostly females or males in a gendered profession, we may find within ourselves knowledges that have been silenced, "knowing" that has been oppressed as we have attempted to survive within a predetermined way of knowing. As with most of us, my first interests as a professional have been for the care and education of children and for my own care and education as a teacher. I was repelled by the apparent control imposed on human beings by the use of behaviorism and profoundly influenced by Piagetian genetic structuralism (1970). The notion that individuals construct their own rules, concepts, and world appealed to my belief in human competence and agency. However, as I further explored the assumptions underlying Piagetian developmental psychology, I came to understand the determinism that is implied. As I have read the work of such authors as Vivian Paley, Shirley Brice Heath, Erica Burman, Lisa Delpit and Jonathan Kozol, and worked with children and adults whose life experiences are different from my own, I have become concerned with social justice and equity for children and adults. Examination of my own beliefs has· revealed a postmodern philosophy (Lyotard, 1984), a view of knowledge as human invention, created by diverse groups in diverse forms dependent on context and circumstances. Although hoping to avoid universals, I agree with the notion that (at least within our current predominately western context) the construction of knowledge is rooted in power relations; the knowledge created by those in power dominates. Increased social justice and equity for both children and adults requires that all forms of knowledge be deconstructed and problematized and that we create avenues from which multiple forms of knowledge can be heard (Kincheloe, 1993).

The Knowledge That We "Know"

The following describes what professionals have considered the knowledge base for the field, views of children and the foundation for educating them. The discussion is not meant to be exhaustive, but to outline simply the philosophical perspectives, events, people, and languages from which we have constructed the dominant view of what we "know."

Our Present Narrative

The history of early childhood education is familiar to all of us in the field. The historic content of the classes that we teach and the textbooks that we use are easily predictable. This traditional narrative, constructed mostly by Euro-American males, usually begins with brief discussions of instinctual child rearing methods during prehistoric times (Osborn, 1991). Without participation in formal training, younger members of a society learned to hunt and gather almost self–sufficiently by four of five and were often considered equal to adults by eight years of age. We have attributed this equality to the simplicity of a primitive life during a particular historical period.

We trace the "progress" of human beings from hunting and gathering, to farming, to constructing early villages. As human functioning advanced through language and cultural complexity, more learning was required of those who were young through imitation of and participation with elders. As villages became cities (Good & Teller, 1969), the need for specializations in trade and record keeping emerged. Between 3000–2000 B.C., schools for males from the upper socioeconomic class were established to teach writing and accounting. As human progress led to city life, children living in the newly emerged cities appeared more helpless and dependent on others to survive.

Within this progressive perspective, the examination of the views of "childhood" has resulted in a debate regarding the treatment of children during ancient periods. DeMause (1974) reports that infanticide was common in ancient cultures. Children who lived earlier in history were more likely to be sexually abused, beaten, abandoned and receive poorer quality care. French (1991) disagrees, proposing that when beliefs about childhood are analyzed in cultural context, history reveals the general tendency toward nurturance. As we explore this debate, the rise of Christianity is most often given credit for a change in attitudes regarding life in general and children in particular. Children were considered an enjoyable and integral part of family life. However, abandonment and infanticide continued to occur. In the 1700s, foundling homes were established in the large cities of Europe, with thousands of children admitted to each institution.

In most texts, we find particular names and events considered pivotal in constructing the field. Plato and Aristotle are among the first given credit for beliefs regarding childhood and a need for education. Aristotle detailed the notion of individual differences in children, suggesting that each child possesses particular skills and talents. Plato proposed education for children under six and, asserting that most parents were not competent to raise children, believed that the state should become responsible (Osborn, 1991). Even today, early childhood educators (and others) praise thinkers such as Aristotle, Plato, and Socrates as providing us with the concepts and methodologies for meaningful teaching. Their ideas are considered dreams that if fulfilled would provide important advances for modern education (Morrison, 1984).

Luther, Comenius, Rousseau, Pestalozzi, Froebel, and Dewey are perhaps the most familiar names in our past philosophical and educational history (Morrison, 1984). Focusing on religious instruction, civil order, and household regulation, Martin Luther (1483-1546) argued that all children should be provided with an education and that everyone should be taught to read the Bible. He included males and females in his plan for compulsory public education (Painter, 1928). Also a minister, John Amos Comenius (1592-1670) spent his life teaching and writing, including the creation of the *Orbis Pictus*, the first children's picture book. In *The School of Infancy*, Comenius proposed that learning in the mother's lap for the first six years of life served to be the root of all knowledge (Osborn, 1991). He believed in the goodness of man, concrete sensory experiences, and that learning followed the order of nature (Comenius, 1967). As described by using the hypothetical child Emile, Jean Jacques Rousseau (1712-1778) believed in natural development, and that education was the process of learning about nature, the reasoned logic of man, and physical objects in the real world. He believed that education was not for vocational training, but for life (Rousseau, 1933). Believing in the work of Rousseau, Johann Heinrick Pestalozzi (1746-1827) used *Emile* as a guide in raising his own son. Although he was not successful in educating his son to read or write, Pestalozzi is credited with developing pedagogical methods that placed the child first (as opposed to the teacher master as controller) and involved the learner in concretely manipulating objects. Pestalozzi also believed that the mother was the best teacher for the child (Anderson, 1970; DeGuimps, 1890). After spending several years studying and teaching with Pestalozzi, Friedrich Wilhelm Froebel (1782-1852) furthered the notion of natural development through his comparison of the child to a seed. The seed would grow into a mature fruit within a "kindergarten/children's garden" type of environment. Not only were Froebel's ideas the foundation for curriculum, teaching methodologies, and the beginning of teacher training, but he placed the concept of play at the forefront of early education. "Play is the purest, most spiritual activity of man at this stage" (Froebel, 1887, p. 55). In early childhood education, the work of John Dewey (1859-1952) is used to support open education and Piagetian constructivism (Morrison, 1984). Dewey has been interpreted as pleading for active learning in which the child engages in physical activities, social interaction, and learns to use tools and objects. The foundation of the curriculum in a democratically run classroom should be the child's interests (Dewey, 1944).

As Bettye Caldwell has written, "Our field represents the applied side of the basic science of child development" (1984, p. 53). We cannot review the history/knowledge of early childhood education without including child development and its parent discipline, developmental psychology. By the nineteenth century, the demand in Europe for scientific legitimacy in all fields dominated and was consistent with the shift following the Enlightenment from religious/philosophical/intuitive to secular/rational/ positivist perspectives. With the publication of *The Origin of Species* by Charles Darwin in 1859, the scientific method and the notion of progressive change were established. Within this context the field of psychology was constructed containing the new science referred to as child development.

Our discussions of development generally focus on the attainment of more advanced stages of thought and action and have been divided into domains; cognitive, social, emotional, physical, linguistic, and so on. Freud, Erikson, and Piaget are examples of those who have contributed to this child development knowledge base and therefore to what we "know" about children. Sigmund Freud, in the construction of the theory of infantile sexuality, focused on the early years of life as fundamental to adult functioning. In a flurry of work in the twentieth century, researchers such as Erik Erikson extended this focus on child development and early experience as they hypothesized stages of growth that would explain the various "domains" of human functioning (Erikson, 1950; Gesell & Ilg, 1949; Mussen, 1970). Jean Piaget proposed that children individually construct their worlds from the inside out, a process that is described as both self–directed and self–regulated. Through the process of equilibration, the maturing child is defined as intellectually constructing and reconstructing understanding, becoming increasingly more able in the use of abstract mental thought and scientific reasoning (Piaget, 1964, 1968, 1970; Inhelder & Piaget, 1958).

During the twentieth century, psychological theory in one form or the other has dominated early childhood education; behaviorism, measurement and habit formation in the 1920s, Freudian theory in the 1930s, normative child psychology in the 1940s and 1950s, and developmental and Piagetian perspectives during the latter half of the century (Silin, 1987). Further, though the science of psychology, we have constructed and observed characteristics believed important to the growth and functioning of the child. These characteristics include self–concept, attachment, motivation, dependency, aggression, and cooperation, just to name a few.

Events around the world and political conditions in the United States have had an effect on the knowledge that we "know." Beginning with

Froebel's kindergarten in Germany, schools for young children were begun all around Europe and the United States (e.g., 1856, first United States private kindergarten, 1873, first United States public kindergarten). On the heels of the Industrial Revolution, individuals concerned with child observation and welfare joined with labor groups whose members wanted factory jobs for adults. By the early 1900s, these groups had with President Theodore Roosevelt established the Children's Bureau and guidelines for child labor laws. Further, the work of G. Stanley Hall in child study signaled the beginning of large organized studies of children. Research centers were established specifically designed to study child development all around the United States (e.g. New York, Connecticut, Iowa). The 1960s focus in the United States on poverty resulted in government funding to provide programs for those individuals, especially children, who were labeled as deprived, low functioning, or somehow lacking in opportunity. The best-known programs, Head Start and Follow Through, were created for early childhood education.

Teaching methods, content, and models of early childhood education emerged. In addition to Froebel's concepts of gifts (objects from God such as physical shapes) and occupations (physical actvities that could be completed with the gifts such as building with blocks), the successful work of Maria Montessori (Maria Montessori, 1967; Mario Montessori, 1976) with street children in Europe gained prominence. In the 1930s and 1940s, Freudian perspectives dominated the construction of the nursery school as an environment whose purposes were to promote social and emotional well-being. The British Infant School and programs such as Summerhill (Neill, 1960) fostered the belief in open education in which children would be allowed to be free for discovery and self-expression through nature and social interaction with others. With the creation of Head Start, models of education that were grounded in particular psychological perspectives emerged during the 1960s and 1970s. As examples, the Direct Instruction Model in Oregon and the Behavior Analysis Model in Kansas represented a behavioral psychological view. The Cognitively Oriented Curriculum in Michigan and the Mathemagenic Activities Program in Georgia represented a cognitive, Piagetian psychological perspective. During the 1980s and early 1990s, the work of early childhood educators focusing on Piagetian constructivism has dominated (See DeVries & Kohlberg, 1987/1990; Kamii, 1993, 1989, 1985, 1982; Kamii & DeVries, 1978/1993, 1980), combined with whole language perspectives (Ferreiro & Teberosky,

1979/1982; Manning & Manning, 1989; Teale & Sulzby, 1986). Analysis of child care environments has also continued, most often based on issues within a child development context. Displaying a compatibility with the Piagetian focus, the most recent sites of exploration are community–based early education programs such as Reggio Amelia (Edwards, Gandini, & Forman, 1993; New, 1991) and a concern for the bilingual education (the term used in the United States) of linguistically diverse young children (Fillmore, 1991; Garcia & McLaughlin, 1995; Kagan & Garcia, 1991).

Consistent with the domination of early childhood by psychological perspectives, the National Association for the Education of Young Children in 1987 published a document entitled *Developmentally Appropriate Practice in Early Childhood Programs Serving Children from Birth to Eight* (Bredekamp, 1987). This document is grounded in developmental psychology, most obviously exhibiting a Piagetian influence. Classrooms all over the United States are currently exploring the potential use of the teaching guidelines provided in the document. Early childhood educators themselves are currently debating the universalist perspective implied by the notion of "appropriate practice."

This history/knowledge has served as our philosophical, psychological, and historical foundation. Only a few of us have questioned the content or origin (See Silin, 1987). Yet, as I have simply presented the content to graduate students from diverse backgrounds, they have questioned this history that we "know":

What is this notion of civilization; why is it better than hunting and gathering; didn't other human beings emerge in their own areas of the world?

Why do White males who appear to be from either Europe or the United States dominate the information?

How do we know that older human beings are more advanced or more sophisticated than younger people? This is hard to argue with because we're all getting older and want to think that it is better than being younger.

My family is from India and we don't go through these stages; my mother says that preadolescence and adolescence are American constructions.

As an African American, I don't believe that psychology has been kind to us. Why should we subject our children to methods of measuring and categorizing people?

Voices of Silent "Knowing"

As we have constructed what we "know " in the field, there are voices that have not been heard, knowledge that has not been part of our history or the decisions that we as professionals have made for others. The most critical voices that are silent in our constructions of early childhood education are the children with whom we work. Our constructions of research have not fostered methods that facilitate hearing their voices. However, a small number of researchers have recognized the importance of sharing in the lives of others as a way of hearing that which has been silenced.

In her work with the Trackton and Roadville communities, Shirley Brice Heath (1983) revealed the diverse language and cultural strengths demonstrated by young children that were not heard or recognized by professionals in schools. Lem is an excellent example. In the African American community of Trackton, Lem was recognized as a competent community member. At 2 and 1/2 years of age, he constructed a story poem about a distant ringing bell that exhibits story formula and poetic balance (p. 170).

"Way
Far
Now
It a church bell
Ringin'
Dey singing'
   ringin'
You hear it?
I hear it
Far
Now"

His multiple stories about trains further illustrate this poetic, creative strength even at the age of four (p. 110):

"Railroad track
Train all big'n black
On dat track, on dat track, on dat track
Ain't no way I can't get back
Back from dat track
Back from train
Big'n black, I be back"

The children who speak through the work of Jonathan Kozol (1991) demonstrate the complexity, ambiguity, and terror of living in the silenced, regulated, poor communities in the United States. The voices of East St. Louis are expressed clearly: "On one side of us you have two chemical corporations ... On the other side are companies incinerating toxic waste. So the trash is comin' at us this direction. The chemicals is comin' from the other. We right in the middle." (the voice of Luther, p. 31) "I love my friends ... I care for them. I hope his mother have another baby. Name her for my friend that's dead." (the voice of Serena about her murdered friend, p. 14) "We have a school in East St. Louis named for Dr. King ... The school is full of sewer water and the doors are locked with chains. Every student in that school is black. It's like a terrible joke on history." (no name provided, p. 35)

Finally, Lisa Delpit (1995) has reminded us of our unvillingness to be silent so that we might hear the voices of those who share in the lives of younger human beings. She describes a Black teacher's thoughts about her White colleagues: "When you're talking to White people they still want it to be their way ... they think they know what's best for everybody, for everybody's children. They won't listen" (p. 21). Kozol reveals the words of a mother in the Chicago South Side as she explains the absurdity of corporate leaders portraying themselves as allies, as listeners: "The same bank presidents who offer gifts to help our segregated schools are the ones who have assured their segregation by redlining neighborhoods ... and who vote against the equalizing plans to give our public schools more money" (p. 81). Even those of us who want to hear multiple voices become so committed to our constructions of how to listen and what to hear that we silence both younger human beings and those in their lives that do not speak our language.

These voices of silent knowing would teach us to examine what we think we know and lead us to explore and respect multiple world–views. Not only have we silenced those who are younger, but we have limited ourselves by conceiving of only one way of hearing or one way of being in the world. Without the critique of what we think we know and the willingness to hear voices that make us uncomfortable, we limit not only those who are silenced, but everyone.

Problematizing What We "Know"

With the acceptance in the 1930s in the United States and European logical positivism, natural–science models finally overshadowed all other forms of human interpretation in the so–called Western world (Morrow, 1994). The belief that science and the scientific method could lead to ultimate truth(s) that could be generalized universally set the stage for the emergence of structuralism in the 1960s. The Kantian theory that there are universal cognitive structures that govern the human mind was embraced by those concerned with human functioning as they accepted Piaget's genetic structuralism (1970). Although individual thought or language is not believed to be specifically controlled by a predetermined universal human system, structuralists are convinced that rules and universal concepts regulate, determine, and constrain human thought and activity. The cognitive structures proposed by Piaget illustrate the perspective. For example, one truth is that all human beings progress toward logical thought. The process is regulated through the creation of cognitive dissonance, explained using the equilibration/disequilibration model. Humans use this process at their own rates and through multiple, diverse experiences, but the result is always either assimilation or accommodation.

During the later half of this century, a number of positions have emerged that oppose structuralist claims. Although positions vary, poststructuralists tend to characterize truth (e.g., reality, knowledge) as subjective, indeterminate, and created by human beings to best fit their understandings of particular contexts (Dews, 1987). Truth is not viewed as existing in a predetermined reality that applies to all human beings. Truths, realities, and knowledges, whether presented as cognitive structures, universal human logic, or stages of development, are considered human constructions. The belief in predetermined truth(s) and knowledge(s) as independent from human creators is considered reductionist and gives the false appearance of a neutral, value–free orientation.

Most recently, some of these theorists have proposed that the truths that are constructed and accepted as legitimate are dependent on the negotiation (or lack of negotiation) of power relationships between various groups of people (Kincheloe, 1991; Lincoln & Guba, 1985). This most radical form of poststructuralism was termed postmodernism by Jean-Francois Lyotard (1984) in his discussion of the decline of modern grand narratives such as Marxism, Freudianism, and functionalism.   Modern narratives—for example the American focus on independence and logic—are considered constructions of truth and knowledge that mask the acquisition and maintenance of power. Postmodernist thinkers have challenged the objectivity of knowledge or language, questioned the view of present thinking and innovation as superior to other periods in time, and interrogated the appropiateness of general world views that are applied to all human beings (Appleby, Hunt, & Jacob, 1994).

Although differing in methodology, two dominant postmodern thinkers are Michel Foucault (1926-1984) and Jacques Derrida (1930-   ). Both are French and became adults in the late 1940s and early 1950s. Pursuing broad experiences around the world, Foucault worked in Sweden, Germany, and California and Derrida taught extensively in the United States. Both believe that truth is a human invention, possibly even a Western illusion. Truth, reality, and knowledge are always changing and constructed by human beings in multiple forms. Language is considered the major avenue for the production of knowledge and is tied to the cultural codes of those who create its forms. Human beings are therefore imprisoned by the language reality created in a particular cultural context (Derrida, 1981).

Language/Discourse and Problematization

Believing that language, which he refers to as discourse, constructs knowledge and consequently limits alternative knowledge forms, Foucault raises the questions:

What knowledges have been excluded?
Whose knowledge has been disqualified as beneath our hierarchical systems?
Whose truths have been hidden through our rhetorical methods?

How have particular groups gained control over others through the construction of discourse knowledges and truths? (Foucault, 1980).

If language practices create "what we think we know," then the forms of discourse that are used to justify knowledge must be analyzed. The ascendance of particular language/knowledge constructions over others creates conditions of power. Discourses are analyzed in terms of their effect, not promises or claims (Sawicki, 1991). For example, the language/knowledge of testing controls teachers, parents, and children in many of our school environments. Foucault's belief that power should be analyzed from the bottom up results in the analysis of history as counter–memory (Hutton, 1993). How have we chosen to write and read history? What has been included? What has been excluded?

Using methods called (1) the archaeology, and (2) the genealogy of knowledge, Foucault constructed research projects that problematized historical constructions such as medicine, sexuality, and mental illness. The archaeology of knowledge is a somewhat structuralist method used by Foucault to study the emergence of a system of thought (Morrow, 1994). Archaeological principles focus on the rules that are used within the studied discourse(s), the specific rules that differentiate one discourse from another, the governance of individual and social action by a discourse, and results in an analysis of the discourse. The purpose is not to reinterpret a discourse, but to systematically describe the discourse as object, to uncover the regularity of practice (Foucault, 1972). For example, the dominant discourse on "motherhood" follows a rule in which mothers are always referred to as the most important human being in a child's life. Women are then governed by this language–induced expectation. In *Madness and Civilization*, Foucault (1965) demonstrated how the dominant discourse of rationalization prevalent during the Enlightenment countered the view of madness as eccentricity. During the Middle Ages, madness was believed to represent divine possession and was tolerated. Following the Enlightenment, people became afraid of those individuals whose behaviors did not follow the rational pattern. Insanity was constructed; conformity was privileged over creativity (Hutton, 1993). Those who conformed, and especially those who created the rules for conformity, gained power over those who deviated.

The genealogy of knowledge is a perspective and method in which knowledge is viewed as rooted in power relations. Genealogy begins by locating a particular practice in the present that represents a discontinuity (Sawicki, 1991). For example, in *Discipline and Punish*, Foucault (1977) asks the question: Since imprisonment had been rejected in the past, how did it come to be accepted as an appropriate form of punishment? Genealogical analysis leads to further questions: What knowledge has been hidden within the construction of imprisonment? Whose knowledges have been disqualified? For example, knowledge of the "delinquent" was oppressed/subjugated as beneath the appropriate level of functioning to be heard. This study marked Foucault's transition from the isolated study of discourse to the social context that is foundational to particular discourse practices (Blanchot, 1989).

Basically, Foucault's focus was not to trace the history of particular concepts, practices, or institutions, but to problematize or reveal the discourse, the rhetoric, the method for representing the world, that was constructed as justification. In an excellent example, Skrtic (1995) has recently used a genealogical method to trace the discourse/knowledge tradition that has shaped and justified the field of special education. Those of us in early childhood education have focused on constructions of the child, the knowledge that psychology has provided to us, and the history of particular educational practices and institutions as related to the child. With the exception of a few discussions (See Silin, 1987, 1995), we have not problematized the discourses that have been used to construct and justify actions in our field. We have not asked questions such as the following:

> *What knowledge has been hidden within the discourse on developmental psychology? Whose knowledge is disqualified as we construct notions of "childhood"?*
> *How is the exclusion and control of younger human beings, subjugated cultures, or subdominant groups like females hidden in the forms of discourse that we use?*

Deconstruction and Reconstruction

Derrida proposed deconstruction as a strategy for reading the written word. Focusing predominately on literature, he has described language as both reflecting and generating power, a mirror of particular ideologies and socially constructed norms. In text, particular words or concepts (signifiers) are certified as truth and attached to particular cultural representations (signified), resulting in the privileging of those forms of being. Deconstructive methods are common in literature and art, but have only recently gained attention as applicable to what is traditionally identified as scientific (Lather, 1991). For example, the word civilization (signifier) is linked to western ways of living (signified), not to forms of African life (Kincheloe, 1993). Power is generated for those who demonstrate western forms of being. More importantly, people who do not match with that which is signified are considered not civilized, savage, deficient, ignorant, or even immoral. Other examples include the construction of the term progress (signifier) as linked to scientific thought (signified), attachment (signifier) as linked to good mothering (signified), innocence and neediness as linked to the child.

Defined in multiple ways, deconstruction is a method of reading and interpreting (the word and/or the world) that reveals hidden meanings, silences, contradictions, and sites of power. The data are historical, current, multidirectional, dialogic, qualitative, quantitative, and unlimited depending on the locations of hidden textual messages. Deconstruction attacks not only the credibility of traditional connections between signifier and signified, but the forms of thinking in which both are embedded. Deconstruction reveals the sites of power generated by the "sign" (Kincheloe, 1993, p. 90), allowing for alternative readings of the world. Deconstruction reveals dominate themes and forms of discourse, unmasking the contradictions and biases in those themes. Deconstruction can be defined as the examination of dominate frames of reference without which the status quo remains unchallenged (Cherryholmes, 1988). Deconstruction fictionalizes hegemonic truth and unlocks the door to multiple possibilities.

Patti Lather (1991) explains evocative parameters of deconstructive inquiry. First, language and reality are recognized as inscriptive rather than descriptive, as subjectively and deeply embedded rather than representing positivist truth. The inquiry recognizes the researcher as a subjective being, attempting to create meaning, to give life to multiple forms of thought. Finally, deconstruction, as with all other forms of research, is viewed as a political act, potentially creating privilege for the researcher. The research represents simply a voice among multiple voices, not the voice of truth (whose existence the deconstructive process would interrogate), but a voice that would be equitably heard, considered, and respected.

Beginning the Journey

For me, this book begins the journey toward a search for reconceptualization, a recognition that our attempts to improve the lives of others through education and care may be modernist constructions through which we have unknowingly further colonized them. If there is even the possibility that our notions of progress and our attempts to help other human beings have actually contributed to their regulation, we must examine our beliefs, actions, and the contexts from which they have emerged. Perhaps we should be asking different questions. Perhaps we should be listening to and envisioning new possibilities. I have come to believe that without multiple forms of critique, our field can only foster dominant perspectives; the field thus functions to silence the voices of diverse others. I also believe that as a field we can deal with and welcome multiple forms of critique and reconceptualization. As individual teachers we have always dealt with ambiguity, recognized the need for open-endedness, and appreciated the multiple lives of the younger human beings with whom we have shared our own lives. We have not wanted to limit others by imposing our world on them.

I do not present this book or its text as a truth, but as an avenue for the construction of new possibilities. I do propose that we do not have to have the concepts of child, or child development, or child–centeredness, or professionalism to function as human beings who openly care about and respect others and that perhaps those concepts do not benefit others as we would hope. I propose that we begin a new journey, an educational course of critique and possibility, an excursion that acknowledges the ever–present existence of human bias and the never ending struggle to conceptualize how we live together and respect each other. We now begin the journey.

Chapter II

The Genealogy of Childhood

To recognize that child is a role is to suspend the assumption that childhood has some absolute, real, transcendent existence beyond the social.

Waksler, 1991, p. 68

To most of us, childhood is a human condition that we have all experienced and see as distinctly different from "adulthood." Most people who live in the United States appear to believe that children are a distinct group who are to be controlled and protected, guided and encouraged to explore. Education, and especially early childhood education , is dominated by the belief that the child is a whole and separate being, relying on adults for guidance toward individual independence. We discuss what children are like, what they need, and who we want them to be. We label them as becoming more independent, competent, or self–reliant. We create special programs, materials, and experiences for them. Some of us dedicate our lives to them either through professional services to them as a group or to the individual children that we raise as our "own." Younger human beings, labeled as "children," are viewed as a distinctly different group of people, a group who must have their decisions made for them, their actions carefully observed and monitored. To a great extent, we have assumed that our beliefs and actions regarding them are warranted and result in benefits to them. We have created the ultimate "Other," a group of human beings not considered able or mature enough to create themselves. We have not analyzed the assumptions and beliefs that underlie our creation. We have accepted and contributed to the discourse/language of "childhood" without question or critique. We have not discussed the possibilities that younger members of society may not all benefit from living within our constructions of "childhood."

When the notion of childhood is questioned, particular reactions are common:

Children are different from adults; how could anyone question those differences and the dependence of very young children on us as adults? We have learned much about children, especially from the field of developmental psychology, and should use that knowledge to improve

their lives. Those who question our knowledge are attempting to throw the baby out with the bath water.
Are you saying that children are just like adults? That idea would cause people in power to eliminate the strides we have made for children, the special programs, protections, and services.

Analysis of the assumptions underlying the construction of the child does open the door to questions from the political right, the political left, and from directions that we have not perceived. However, by questioning our construction of the child, we also open the dialogue to younger members of society, rather than requiring that they live within our constructions of them. Critical analysis can result in greater possibilities, in liberation, and in hope.

The purposes of this chapter are to problematize the notion of "childhood" as a predetermined human condition (Castel, 1994; Foucault, 1977) and to examine how our constructions of the "child" serve to limit and devalue the multiple ways in which we may learn to know children (Merleau-Ponty, 1964; Silin, 1987). Not only is childhood as an historical/political construction examined, but questions such as the following are addressed:

How have the younger members of human society come to be considered as separate and qualitatively distinct from those who are older?
What are the discourse practices that have dominated the construction of the child?
Whose knowledge has been hidden or disqualified within these discourses?
Who has gained power within the discourses of childhood?

Childhood as Western and Modern

As previously discussed, the philosophical perspectives and history that have dominated our constructions of life have been Euro-American, western and to some extent controlled by educated, white, middle, and upper class males. So to-with the history and construction of childhood as a universal human condition. The belief in childhood as a unique and distinct period of humanity appears to have largely emerged in the Enlightenment and Modern historical periods. The beliefs and discourse practices of these periods thus become integral components of a genealogy of childhood.

Enlightenment History

During the seventeenth and eighteenth century Enlightenment, also referred to as the Age of Reason, European intellectuals believed that all knowledge (truth) would be discovered through reason, resulting in freedom and happiness. Intellectual thought fused concepts of God with reason, nature, and man. This belief in reason was rooted in the Greek focus on reason and the mind, most often referred to in discussions of the intellectual abilities of man advanced by Socrates. As power was consolidated by the Romans over the Greeks, a Greco–Roman culture emerged that integrated the concern for reason and the mind with Roman perspectives. The Greco–Roman culture eventually lost vitality. Various religious doctrines of personal salvation developed, with Christianity winning the greatest number of converts.

Christians interpreted Greek and Roman philosophy as pagan, yet were faced with converts who were not willing to give up pagan beliefs entirely. While continuing to destroy literature that was in Christian judgment considered the most immoral, Christians revised other Greco-Roman literature to support their philosophy and views of faith. For example, in the thirteenth century, Thomas Aquinas revised a newly found manuscript by Aristotle to be consistent with Christian philosophy. Thus, Greek focus on reason and the mind was incorporated into Christian theology.

By the sixteenth century, a philosophically divided Europe emerged. Europeans found themselves in political turmoil, especially in Italy. Scholars grew interested in the original, unrevised classics. The Christian church was divided as shown by the impact of Martin Luther. Concern that the European community shared no common thought, resulted in a search for common ground. In 1625, Hugo Grotius, a Dutch scholar, proposed the existence of natural law, universal rules of nature that were independent of Christian theology and which could be used to govern relations between diverse groups. Within this context, a universalist belief in science emerged that continues to dominate western thought (Macpherson, 1962).

Science. Until around the seventeenth century, science was considered to be a passive observation of the natural world (Wolf, 1981). Reconceptions of science began in a variety of contexts and events including the pursuit of man and nature by Renaissance artists, Spanish and

Portuguese explorations of Africa and the Middle East, the use of
mathematical theories in southern Germany for mining, and the
development of mathematical skills for use in the wars generated by the
Protestant Reformation. The work of Francis Bacon in England, René
Descartes in France, and Galileo Galilei in Italy received attention.
Although the two did not generally agree philosophically, both Bacon and
Descartes believed that science could improve life and that science and
theology were separate. Descartes proposed that mind and matter were
separate, leading to the conceptualization of the world as a system with two
domains: (1) the internal, individual mind; and (2) the objective world of
nature. Galileo supported the notion of an impersonal exploration of nature
(and interpreted nature to be mathematics). Further supported by most
scientists, this Cartesian dualism resulted in the belief in objective, usually
dichotomous, ways of thinking. Human perception and reality were
considered distinct and separate. If scientists isolated themselves from
perception and established objective reality, scientific discoveries would
result (Kincheloe, 1991; Lavine, 1984; Lowe, 1982). One example of an
objectively determined scientific discovery was the notion of cause and
effect, the accuracy of prediction if all conditions are understood.

Religion. The beginning of modern science posed threats to the
Christian church. First, although many of the scientists were Christians
themselves they questioned some Christian views as not upheld under the
scientific test of reason. Second, at the time that natural laws were
proposed, a definition for "natural religion" also developed. Natural
religion professed that there were certain beliefs that are so obvious that all
men of reason would accept them. The belief in one God was an example
of a reasoned natural belief, a view that was accepted by all forms of
Christianity. A group called Deists, who believed in universal natural
religion through reason, challenged Christianity. Deists did not believe that
God would set aside natural laws to reveal religious doctrine in a book such
as the *Bible*. Jean-Jacques Rousseau professed his belief in Deism in the
book *Emile* as part of discussions of the individual, autonomous man;
individuals would not be separated from God by religious artifacts such as
the *Bible*. Although spreading, Deism met with Christian attacks through
the use of civil judgments, censorship, book bannings, and even the death
penalty.

Enlightenment Discourse

This concept of natural law manifested itself in the search for *universal human truths*, most strongly supported by David Hume. Human nature was considered natural and constant, understood and controllable through universal principles, and discoverable through *reason* and the newly emerging *scientific* tools. Consistent with the separation of mind and matter proposed by Descartes, a discourse of *oppositional dichotomy* emerged as descriptions of human understanding flourished. "All the perceptions of the human mind resolve themselves into two distinct kinds, which I shall call IMPRESSIONS and IDEAS" (original author's capitalizations, Hume, 1982, p. 15). Further, *individualism* permeated both religion and science with the focus on the moral and reasoning individual. John Locke chose to use Newton's scientific method to determine the universals of human nature. From this perspective, he came to believe that all knowledge is derived through *experience* and reflection, an epistemology of experience. To improve man, improve the environment in which experience takes place.

Enlightenment rationalist philosophers formulated the notion of *progress*, man advancing in a predetermined, desirable direction. The Greeks, Romans, or Renaissance Europeans did not hold to or even consider the idea. Francis Bacon, however, contended that the Greeks and Romans were actually like children of civilization. His own generation had accumulated the greatest amount of knowledge and scientific information. Supporting Bacon's perspective, Bernard Fontenelle asserted that progress is man's destiny and will always lead to better conditions (Bury, 1932). Because knowledge is progressive, advances will occur independent of particular individuals.

As enlightenment philosophy faced challenges, the late eighteenth to mid-nineteenth century can be characterized as a period of *counterdiscourse*. Romanticism, the revolt against reason, science, order, and control manifested itself most clearly in the arts, but was also evident in social, political, and moral reform. Jean-Jacques Rousseau's earlier belief in the natural goodness of man previewed the coming romantic perspective. The literature of Germany and England, however, served as the origin of romantic criticism. Examples include the gothic novel that blended evil and horror with natural beauty and the poetry of William Wordsworth and Samuel Coleridge. Bodies of literature that were just being formed during the time period (e.g., United States, Belgium, Ireland) were so strongly influenced by the focus on feelings and political liberalism that they have remained basically Romantic to this day. Accepting man as an irrational animal, Romanticism emphasized individuality, especially through self–expression and accepted individual expression without the necessity of following a "rational" form.

Modernization

Most often, modernization is associated with industrialization, continuous change, and a focus on scientific thought (Weiner, 1966). The nineteenth and twentieth centuries have been periods of modernization in Europe and the United States, beginning with the Industrial Revolution in England. Consistent with enlightenment views of progress, modern thought asserts that human beings are moving toward increasingly more advanced civilizations. As societies are modernized, two processes occur: (a) secularization, organizing activities around impersonal, utilitarian values; and (b) individualization, rational choice by independent people. Knowledge is viewed as accelerated, advanced, and most appropriately applied to technology with the goal of maximizing productivity and efficiency. Machines often appear as symbols of modernization, whether as signs of increased production, or as signs of science replacing superstition (Anderson, 1966). Change is believed to be universal and expected by those who are more advanced; less primitive societies are more likely to be modern in thought and action. Although conflict is seen as unavoidable as civilizations are modernized, when more advanced stages of modernization occur, conflict will decrease.

Empirically based science and technology are the foundation for modern perspectives. Partly attributable to the belief in progress, a moral optimism has dominated scientific activity over the last 200 years. Progress in science would either benefit humanity or have no impact. This faith in science has been characterized as positivism (Lincoln & Guba, 1985). Views of the world that have generally dominated positivist science include the belief in universal truths (e.g., laws, knowledge, facts, reality) and the acceptance of science, especially the objective scientific method as the way to reveal those truths. Modernist science is believed to uncover universal truths that are applicable to all human beings and improve life for everyone.

Modernist Discourse

Obvious in both descriptions of modern societies and in what those who live in industrialized nations see and hear daily is a form of the Enlightenment language of *progress*. The discourse of progress has not only been accepted but is universally applied to knowledge, societies, and even individuals. Modern man claims to be more advanced in all ways, intellectually, morally, and technologically, just to name a few. Further, the dualistic, often *dichotomous, language and thought* of the Age of Reason is fostered. As examples, societies are considered either primitive or modern; science is objective while other fields are not. The notion of *universal truth* that can be scientifically determined dominates discourse. Human beings can find the answers, can control the environment. The reality that governs people can be scientifically revealed. To be truly modern, an *individual* is self–controlled, well contained, and emotionally balanced, so that the complexities of the world are fully integrated. The modern focus (especially in the United States) is on the individual, from growth or deficiency, to strengths and weaknesses. The individual is held responsible for his/her successes and failures, intellect, physical health, and religious salvation. The individual is both in charge and at fault.

Childhood as Construction

Part of both Enlightenment and Modernist discourses is the notion that younger human beings represent a unique human condition called "childhood":

What then is meant by the child (or childhood) as construction? Or the child as cultural invention?

We know that there are 7-year-olds, 5-year-olds, 2-year-olds, and even infants all around us. Certainly, they are actual, real children, not ideas constructed by adults; but what is meant by the notion of the "real child"?

What does it mean when we place the label "child" on a 6-year-old or a 3-year-old?

Is this label beneficial to the person?

Is the label ever harmful?

As early childhood educators, we have recognized that the concept of child has changed over time and in different historical contexts. This changing concept has generally been interpreted as progressively more complete and adding to our understanding of younger members of society. Consistent with Enlightenment views of progress, our Euro-American belief concerning children is that we have learned what they are like, especially those of us who are childhood experts. We can describe how they grow, change, and think, and the types of environments that are best for them. In the twentieth century, we define childhood as a time of life that is distinct from adulthood and qualitatively different in thought and ability. Most of us are sure of our belief that childhood is a human universal truth that can be defined and interpreted.

Cross-cultural analysis, however, reveals diverse constructions of childhood, rooted in the philosophical and political context of life. As examples, in Confucian China, a young person was expected to display good conscience and behavioral control as soon as he/she was able to walk and talk. Even toddlers were expected to display respectful responses and actions. Play was not appropriate (Dardess, 1991). Similarly, in nineteenth century Australia, an economic depression in the early 1800s that was followed by the chaotic events of the 1850s gold rush, led the middle class to become greatly concerned with social order. Out of this concern for organization and control, methods for institutionalizing children emerged in the form of reformatories, orphanages, and industrial schools (Gordon, 1991). Solberg (1990) has shown how constructions of age are changing for Norwegian children as they become part of family work activities and perceptions of equality. The children of Trackton (Heath, 1983) in the Carolinas clearly demonstrated language skills that positivist research would characterize as too advanced for their age level.

Even within similar cultural contexts, Kessen (1979) points out that different images of children have been invented by different theorists. Freud found a child who was constructed through sexual desire; Piaget observed a child formed through adaptation; Skinner found "a baby in a box" (p. 28). Although Locke was a bachelor and Rousseau sent each of his five children to a foundling home at birth, each described a theory that has contributed to the invention of the modern child. Keniston (1976) has noted a tendency for the human participant in each historical age to "freeze its own unique experience into an ahistorical vision of Life-in-General" (p.

144). In our constructions of the child, this ahistorical, overgeneralized vision has dominated.

Finally, and most importantly for a genealogy of childhood, constructivist (Lincoln & Guba, 1985) and critical (Agger, 1991; McCarthy, 1991; Poster, 1989) philosophical perspectives would suggest that the concept of child does not represent a universal human truth, but a category created through language that may actually limit and control the lives of those who are "constructed" (and potentially those who are part of their lives). Schwartz and Ogilvy (1979) described belief systems asserting that realities are constructions of the human mind. Constructivist thought, the contemporary label for these complex, indeterminate perspectives, characterizes reality (e.g., truth, knowledge, labels for human beings) as subjective, created by human beings to best fit their perceptions of particular social contexts, and subject to continual revision. All constructions are value laden, none independent from the theories and values of the constructor and his/her social group (Lincoln & Guba, 1985). Constructivist perspectives would suggest that the notion of "child" is a social creation, not an independent reality, created by human beings in a particular time and context. Critical theory supports the notion of a social, value laden construction, focusing on the multiple forms of human domination that result (Golding, 1992; Laclau, 1990; Morrow, 1994). Based on a critical constructivist philosophy, historical context and religion, the arts, and science all appear to have contributed to our construction of the child.

Created in History

Greek and Roman histories reveal some reference to younger members of society, especially in the work of Plato and Aristotle, who were concerned about the education of boys for the good of the state (French, 1991). Aristotle proposed that each student was an individual with different talents and abilities. Plato believed that parents were not qualified to deal with offspring and that all children should be turned over to the government and placed in state nurseries (Osborn, 1991). Aeschylus referred to the difficulty in discovering the meaning of a baby's cry; and Aristophanes discussed a father who handled his son's toilet training. Generally, however, the attention to younger members of society during the Greek and Roman periods did not result in the creation of a separate group of people or any kind of exploration for understanding. Most often references appear to deal with control issues, especially regarding boys.

As part of the construction of multiple gods, however, the "child god" was common in ancient mythology (Jung & Kerenyi, 1963; Kennedy, 1988) and represented existence in the world in a different manner than adults. This infant or young child was usually of divine origin, survived persecution, and exhibited extraordinary powers. During the medieval period, Christianity psychologized this image of the primordial child. The image of a little child appeared in the Gospels. Christianity asserted the specialness of an ordinary child and the distinction from the adults around "him" (Fuller, 1979, p. 85). By the fifteenth century, the Franciscan tradition had fully supported the religious notion of the "holy innocent" child, consistent with the naturalist perspective of the times. Although challenged by the Renaissance revival of classical texts, Christianity demanded that adults "become as a little child" (Kennedy, p. 125), faithful and dependent on God as the parent. Construction of the child god dominated religious thought.

Although conflicting accounts have emerged including the influence of religion as described above, in medieval Europe, younger members of society were generally not considered distinct from others (Nicholas, 1991). All humans passed through the "ages of life" (Aries, 1965, p. 23), measured generally in years. "Ages of life" to some extent corresponded to social function, and had no psychological or maturational determinants. Mortality was so high that most did not live through all ages. Younger members of society were not necessarily ignored or neglected, but were simply treated as all others were treated (Block, 1995). Aries (1962) points out that, independent of religious doctrine, childhood did not exist during the medieval period. Our concern for the construction of childhood would not have been a discussable issue. Dependence at the beginning of life might last only 6 or 7 years or as many as 25 or 30 years. Males of all ages learned the same content in medieval schools, most often the content necessary for service in a priestly order. Memorization was the dominant method for learning, with reading as a supplementary tool for use when the memory failed. Other learning usually took place in homes through apprenticeships. The age for beginning apprenticeships varied and was not considered an issue. The work continued until the apprentice became skilled enough to live independently. Younger and older people shared in the same world and were not categorized as different from each other.

The interpretation of how children were treated during differing historical time periods has generated much debate. In his seminal work on the construction of child, *Centuries of Childhood*, Aries (1962) came to the conclusion that the French child of the Middle Ages to the eighteenth century was simply treated as a small adult. Upon being weaned, children became part of the adult community, sharing in its advantages and disadvantages. He did not believe that this nonexistence as a separate group of people lead to neglect or mistreatment; children were viewed just like everyone else. The psychohistorian Lloyd de Mause (1974) strongly disagreed with Aries' interpretations by proposing that history for children is a nightmare, revealing beatings, starvation, terrorization, and sexual abuse. The determination reached by de Mause is that the lives of children have improved with each generation only as parents have progressively learned to do a better job in raising their offspring. S. Marshall's (1991) analysis of sixteenth and seventeenth century Holland and Germany revealed that one-third of all infants died, leading to the conclusion that successful childbirth was considered joyous. Polakow (1982), however, has written that the children of eighteenth century France were regularly abandoned and commonly sent to wet nurses for the first 2 to 4 years. Perhaps the debate actually reveals author biases toward either the separation of children and adults or the tendency to consider everyone together as humanity.

The construction of the child as separate and distinct from the adult took place between the thirteenth and seventeenth centuries (Aries, 1962). The dominant forces in this construction of child were the Christian church and the emphasis on reason during the Enlightenment. Reason supported the belief in classification, order, and hierarchy, already governing the church. Further, most moral theologians accepted the Cartesian view that mind and matter are separate. With the Christian focus on the individual soul and the belief that everyone is a creature of God, the clergy created a group that in their view needed protection from a corrupt society and also reformation for themselves. To protect and control, a group must first be identified (Block, 1995). The school, which had in the past served all people together in mixed groups, became the perfect vehicle for the construction, protection, and reformation of the child. The school served both the goal of separating the group from the contamination of the outside world and that of controlling the direction of life. In the view of the clergy at the prominent Port-Royal school, "All the apertures of the cage must be closed

... A few bars will be left open ... this is what is done with nightingales to make them sing and with parrots to teach them to talk" (Aries, p. 114). Children, like parrots and nightingales, were to be isolated from the rest of the world and regulated through a controlled exposure.

Perspectives that were both consistent with enlightenment philosophy and that served the purposes of the clergy were fostered through this educational separation of children from adults. For example, the concept of "graded classes" was created to protect those who were younger in years from those who were older and may have seen more of the debased world. This "separating children according to age and capacity" (Aries, 1962, p. 176) was also consistent with the newly constructed science of progress. In accordance with Fontenelle's belief that progress is man's destiny, reason would support the idea that the individual human being is progressing. Those who are at different points in their progress should not be together. Until this time period, younger members of society dressed the same as men and women. By the seventeenth century, middle- and upper–class children (those who were most likely to be placed in schools) were expected to wear particular outfits to indicate their age group. The clergy defined childhood through the construction of school activities and ways of functioning.

A mass of literature about children from the western world has been generated during the nineteenth and twentieth centuries, the Modern Age. The positivist view of science that has grounded modernization has taken the child, created by the church, and psychologized and biologized that child. The universal condition of childhood can be described, interpreted, and influenced. The individual is tested, examined, and appropriate experiences prescribed. We believe that we know what children are like, what we can expect at various ages, and how we should differentiate our treatment of them. We have fully accepted the scientific notion of the child following "the most current knowledge of teaching and learning, as derived from theory, research, and practice" (Bredekamp, 1987, p. 68). Schooling has continued to construct the child, even as we decide what the child must know as he/she enters school. We continue to place at the center of our concerns, child protection and the determination of what children should know and how they should behave.

* knowledge is based on natural phenomena

Imagined through Art/Literature

Models of childhood are created in multiple ways, even through the eyes of those who create art and literature. Further, the art and literature of a time can provide messages regarding society that are otherwise silent. As most of us know, medieval art portrayed children as small adults, with adult features and body proportions. Although some have hypothesized that the artists of the period were unskilled and could only reproduce the adult likeness, the most convincing explanation is that they were highly influenced by the philosophy of the time (Cleverley & Phillips, 1986). Children were very much part of the adult world. Human philosophy, rather than limited artistic ability, explains child representation. By the thirteenth century, artists began to represent children in three ways: as angels, with adolescent angels commonly featured; as the clothed infant Jesus; and as the naked child. Used as an artistic symbol throughout the ages, the naked, sexless child represented the soul of a dead person. "The dying man breathes the child out through his mouth in a symbolic representation of the soul's departure" (Aries, 1962, p. 36).

As children were more commonly represented in art, they were pictured in the variety of life activities shared with adults. By the seventeenth century, both family and individual child portraits were common and holy children (e.g., saints) were often painted. For the past 150–200 years, children have, however, generally been separated from adults in artistic representation (Aries, 1962).

Before the romantic revolt, children were generally absent from literature (with the exception of small parts in such works as Elizabethan lyrics). Through the work of William Blake, William Wordsworth, and Charles Dickens, a literary interest in children was generated. Children were represented as helpless and innocent, either symbolizing hope or a life that is better off dead. The late nineteenth century artist often felt alienated and perceived a diminishing audience. The inclusion of particular views of the child may have represented the isolation and vulnerability of the artist within an increasingly more scientific context. Although this literature has contributed to the construction of the child, the symbol may actually represent artistic response to a changing society. For example, Little Nell or Tiny Tim may not have actually represented realistic portraits of British children for Charles Dickens or anyone else. "The depiction of a child in many branches of art might not always have been intended to be realistic, but rather symbolic of such things as innocence, purity, and helplessness"

(Cleverley & Phillips, 1986, p. 145). However, whether intended or not, these representation have been associated with living human beings.

Biography has also revealed particular views of the world in certain time periods. The childhoods of prominent men and women have been depicted differently dependent on the ideal view of childhood in the biographer's background. Childhoods of the same persons have been represented in different ways by different biographers from different time periods. The bias toward particular views of the child are so strong that the writing of a biography can be dated based on the description of the life of the child found in the work. The description of childhoods in biographies has become an indicator of the background of the author, rather than the actual childhood of the person whose story is told (Cleverley & Phillips, 1986).

Constructed by Science

The focus on objective reason promoted by Bacon and Descartes was fully applied to human beings in the new science of psychology, the field with perhaps the greatest impact on the construction of the child. Through psychology, the positivist assumptions dominating nineteenth and twentieth century science have been applied to human beings of all ages. If appropriate questions were asked, experiments and observations conducted, and objective conclusions drawn, the "truths" about human mental functioning could be determined.

Although diary studies had been previously conducted by women (Bradley, 1989), Charles Darwin has been historically considered the author of the first child study which he also completed using a diary format (Riley, 1983; Rose, 1985; Walkerdine & Lucey, 1989). In Darwin's study, as in the version of developmental psychology that emerged in the twentieth century, the infant was observed as an independent biological organism. The purposes of these early studies were to reveal the origins of the adult mind. Children were viewed as primitives, as savages. The modern psychologist of the late nineteenth century was to embrace the "spirit of positive science" and "study mind in its simplest form" (Burman, 1994, p. 11). Darwin's (1859) theory actually emphasized variability. He did not endorse the recapitulationist perspective that the stages of human evolution are revealed in the child. Darwin did, however endorse aspects of Lamarckism in assuming linear, progressive human change (Burman,

1994; Morss, 1990). The environment was established for the acceptance of stage theories of development.

With rapid industrialization in the late nineteenth century came social upheaval. The upper class considered increasingly–evident slums and a population with poor health to be indicators of a poor–quality population. Again consistent with the dualistic views of the world, in 1875 Francis Galton posed the nature/nurture question. Heredity versus environment, the empiricist issue that has grounded the construction of most psychological research, became the foundation for regulating those individuals in the population who were considered of poor quality. To control unruly and unkempt elements, individuals must be identified who could be of poor quality (Burman, 1994). Observation and mental testing emerged as the avenues for the scientific control of the social order. People were tested as they entered the United States, in the military, in hospitals, prisons, and schools (Gould, 1981). The younger members of society, those constructed as "child," became one of the largest groups to be identified as recipients and objects of this scientific gaze (Burman, 1994). Within this gaze, children have been identified as normal or abnormal, competent or incompetent, intelligent or slow.

Discourse Practices of Childhood

This history reveals particular themes that have dominated discourse surrounding the construction of the Western child: existence, individuality, universality, progression, and determination by experience, just to name a few. These discourse practices have been used to justify, signify, and create what is meant by the notion of child. The discourse of progress and the language of experience will be analyzed in detail in the following chapters because the depth of an entire chapter is necessary for thorough examination. Three additional rules of discourse will be discussed here, rules that have become so much a part of our society that we do not question the power that they generate. First and most obvious is the assumption that the child exists and is separate from the adult, a dichotomous distinction. Second, is the focus on the individual self–contained human being, whether child or adult. This individual being is believed to possess independent reasoning ability and a soul that must be saved. Finally, the child is constructed through positivist science, a belief that there exists a "child truth," a predetermined reality that, when uncovered, explains the true nature of the younger human being. One cannot simply accept these discourse practices, but must critique them for the knowledge that is privileged and the power that is denied within their use.

Child/Adult Dichotomy

We have constructed a unique state of humanness, the condition of being a child. The condition is that of being qualitatively distinct from the older members of human society. The child depends on the adult not only for food, nurturing, and care, but to learn how to function in the adult world. We can trace this construction most obviously to the Cartesian notion of the separation of mind and matter and the resultant discourse of dichotomies fostered in both the enlightenment and modern periods. Even the romantic counterdiscourse assumes oppositional division, irrational as opposed to rational, feelings as opposed to thoughts. Dominating the early construction of child through the creation of graded schooling, the Christian church also promoted this dualistic perspective by referring to children as innocent, faithful, and dependent, or sinful and corrupt. Controlling more recent constructions of child, the self–proclaimed science of psychology has created the child who is either normal or abnormal, intelligent or slow.

Children are described today as innocent, weak, needy, lacking (in skill or knowledge), immature, fearful, savage, vulnerable, undefined, or open-ended, as opposed to adults who are intelligent, strong, competent, mature, civilized, and in control. Children are the "Other" than the adult. Older members of society have defined the child as the "not me." Younger members of a society may require advocates within the general population if for no other reason than their size. However, they may not actually benefit from this dichotomous distinction. We must ask the questions: Whose knowledge is hidden or disqualified within this dichotomous child/adult construction? Who has gained power?

Hidden/disqualified knowledge. Two of the most common child descriptors illustrate the ways in which the knowledge possessed by younger members of society is denied. These signs that are used to construct the child are the "innocent" and the "needy." The discourse of innocence most obviously implies lack of knowledge or ignorance, as opposed to adults who are not innocent but are intelligent. Silin (1995) illustrates the problem with this innocence/intelligence dichotomy when human beings are faced with illness and death. The adult is no longer all–

knowing when confronted with loss and separation. Death calls to question the certainty of adult knowledge. Further, when someone is viewed as innocent and therefore ignorant, deficiency is inferred. Knowledge is either considered nonexistent or of poor quality. This innocence requires that access to additional knowledge be withheld or controlled with only "safe" knowledge being allowed. Observation and supervision are required to insure this limited access. Psychological surveillance (Walkerdine, 1984) is justified for the protection of the innocent child. Younger human beings are no longer agents in their own world, but those who must be limited and regulated.

Woodhead (1990) discusses the assumptions underlying the notion of childhood needs, a discourse common to society, psychologists, the religious community, and early childhood professionals. We decide what the "needs" of children are and create programs to meet those needs. Woodhead points out that we have either determined those needs through a questionable positivist science or have treated biased, value–laden philosophies of human life as if they were without bias and universally appropriate to everyone. For example, most research in child care has assumed that one consistent caregiver is necessary for healthy human attachment without the recognition that children can become oriented to diverse patterns of interaction and human relationships. In many cultures, the younger members of society interact with 5 to 10 caregivers and live lives that are mentally healthy (Smith, 1980). Further, the discourse of child needs implies that certain human beings can actually identify the needs of others, creating an authoritative knowledge that is controlled by a particular group and is imposed on another. Older human beings (and often a particular expert group) will decide for young people exactly what life will be like, a practice that has been referred to as imperialism (Cahan, Mechling, Sutton-Smith, & White, 1993). Originating with adults, child–rearing manuals, bedtime stories, literature, and mass-media impose on children a particular knowledge that dictates need. Very little evidence exists for the presence of child discourse and knowledge in society. Younger human beings are not heard without the filter of those who are older. Imperialist adult practices silence children with the message that they are not competent to determine their own needs. Child knowledge is not only disqualified, but its existence denied. Additionally, a discourse of child need disqualifies the knowledge of those "adults" who do not agree with the dialogue (for cultural or other reasons).

Although well meaning, child advocates have without critique constructed a universal needy child who must be protected. These attempts to protect have been both beneficial and harmful. For example, child labor laws did remove younger members of society from unsafe, unhealthy conditions—a goal, by the way, that we might have for all members of society. These laws, however, also removed those that would be considered older children from jobs whose significant social contributions had allowed them to feel and be part of human society. The knowledge, skills, and strengths of people between the ages of 5 or 6 to 15 or 16 are denied; we look for ways to entertain them, teach them sports, and keep them out of trouble. They are viewed as without knowledge unless tied to adults. Further, to a lesser extent, this universally needy child denies the knowledge that families construct together, yielding to experts who tell parents how to meet the needs of their children (Silin, 1995).

The discourse of child needs oversimplifies human society and gives the impression that older human beings actually possess the knowledge of other complex humans. Our uncertainty concerning ourselves and others and our continued denial of the political, contextual, and historical nature of human life is concealed through this discourse. For example, a colleague recently said, "We can't deny that all children need to learn to read." Do all human beings, all around the world, in all contexts actually need to learn to read? What do we mean by reading? Should this reading be privileged over other forms of knowledge (Banks, 1993)? How has our history shaped his statement? Does being a highly educated person bias the colleague's beliefs? In this example, focusing on child needs can actually perpetuate dominant pedagogies, and limit other learning possibilities. "Our understanding and respect for childhood might be better served if 'children's needs' were outlawed from future professional discourse, policy recommendations and popular psychology" (Woodhead, 1990, p. 60).

Power production. The construction of child, and especially the dichotomous creation of child versus adult, results in an implicit form of subjugation. Younger human beings are constructed as objects of control. An example can be found in the statement that "Children are our greatest natural resource." This language places a group of human beings into the same category as none human objects like trees, water, and food. A group of human beings are placed into the position of being nationally owned and for use by others. Conditions for control are created because children are constructed as separate (Block, 1995). Living within adult constructions of them, children are denied the power to speak for themselves. The construction of child as a group is simply the continuation of the monocultural enlightenment view exhibited by the European elite in the creation of the poor, women, and the mentally ill as subordinate groups, those who like animals are not equal to the superior group.

Burman (1994) illustrates how the construction of child is used to perpetuate a colonialist power perspective. Charitable agencies advertise for donations to "guarantee" a childhood for children of the "Third World." This perspective uses younger human beings to deny the imperialism that leads to poverty, and perpetuates the notion that people in poverty are responsible for the condition. The strength and agency of a group of children and families are denied and the perception that "First World" countries are the saviors is fostered. The use of childhood creates a perspective in which we can deny the political question regarding our role in subjugating others. We do not ask what we are doing that contributes to the conditions in which people find themselves.

The dichotomous construction of child gives adults the power. The child is viewed as weak, to be protected, innocent, and lacking in experience. Adults are strong, wise, mature, intelligent, and experienced. The characteristics that have been imposed on the child are applied to adults who are some how deficient or lacking when we refer to them as childish, immature, or dependent. The construction of "child" has resulted in the generation of total power for those who are created as "adults."

Individual and Self-Contained

The construction of the "individual" child parallels the creation of the "individual" human being, rooted in the singular Greek focus on reason and the mind, and fostered in the Cartesian separation of mind and matter. Descartes conceptualized two domains, the individual mind and the world of nature. Rousseau discussed the individual, autonomous man as the Christian church expressed concern for the individual soul. Even Romanticism emphasized individuality. Darwin observed the child as an independent organism. The growing field of psychology observed, tested, and judged individuals. In the post war United States, the language of egalitarianism emphasized the development of autonomy and democratic child rearing. Children were encouraged to be independent. James Hymes well illustrated the individualistic point of view in stating, "In America, we like independent little fellows" (Hymes, 1955, 108). Individualism has appeared in the philosophy of monetarism, the notion that people function independently and competitively, that cooperation or other social forms are not natural human characteristics (Macpherson, 1962). As this rational, free, isolated, individual model has emerged, the philosophy has been universally applied to the construction of childhood, resulting in further limitations placed on younger human beings.

Hidden/disqualified knowledge. Foucault (1977, 1978) has discussed the problem with positioning ourselves or other human beings as individual, self–contained agents. We construct a view of ourselves (or the children that we have created) as presocial with innate characteristics such as intelligence or cleverness. The complexity and ambiguity of being human is denied. Living within this individual construction, human beings render themselves incapable of recognizing the "regimes of Truth" that are constructed through language and in society's institutions (Walkerdine, 1987, p. 122). An example of this limit on knowledge is Kohlberg's (1976) theory of moral reasoning. Based on the work of Piaget, Kohlberg proposed three levels, containing six stages, of progress: premoralism, conformism, and individual principled morality. The sixth stage clearly illustrates the "western ideology of individualism" (Burman, 1994, p. 182), even suggesting that individuals like Jesus in the Christian religion displayed this stage of moral reasoning. Possibly without realizing, Kohlberg perpetuated the dominant knowledge, the hegemony of individualism. Recognizing that Kohlberg's work had been with males, Carol Gilligan (1982) conducted research with females, demonstrating that completely different moral perspectives existed. Further, Kagan's (1984) work in diverse cultures has revealed that in some social contexts the highest level of morality is respect for elders, the avoidance of conflict, and the development of harmonious social relations, a form of moral knowledge that almost entirely eliminates the construction of human beings as individuals. When younger human beings are viewed strictly as individuals, the knowledge that is created as part of a group, or multiple cultural, family, or even classroom groups, is denied.

Focusing on the individual child as the social unit masks gender, class, and cultural knowledge. An experience that most teacher educators may find familiar is the constant focus of preservice teachers on the individual child. In response to our concern with issues of multiculturalism, the future teacher continually states, "I will treat all the children in my classroom as individuals, with individual differences in strengths and abilities." This perspective disavows political knowledge, the reality of power issues within society and the construction of schooling, and the group histories and diverse knowledges within which individuals are embedded. For example, if the knowledge requirements in schools were changed from Eurocentric to Afrocentric content, the "behavior" of different individual children might be changed, perhaps even reversed.

Finally, the construction of the individual as the dominant unit of social function actually privileges egocentric, independent experience. Ward (1920) described individual experience as the foundation for interpreting the experience of others. Piaget characterized young human beings as lacking in the ability to understand the experiences, and we could use the word knowledges, of others. In whole language and child-centered approaches to learning, the construction of meaning by the individual is paramount. The notion that knowledge is an individual construction, whether originating with the individual or a group, limits and disqualifies diverse forms of knowledge for both younger and older human beings.

Power production. Perhaps the most obvious way in which power is generated through the language of individualism is the power of one culture over another. Some cultures, and consequently the children representing those groups, do not believe in the autonomous, self-contained individual. The behavior, knowledge, and beliefs associated with individualism will not be valued or exhibited by all children. When institutions, such as schools, favor individualism over multiple views of human beings, a cultural elitism emerges for those younger human beings who are part of the group that values autonomy. These children acquire more power because they "fit" our individualistic construction.

The "priority of the individual" has placed the responsibility for all events of the world on the independent human being. No other agency, whether a theoretical God, fate, chance, or circumstance, is responsible (Kessen, 1993, p. 226). The cause is always within the person. If a younger member of society has difficulty with mathematics, we diagnose the internal problem and remediate the individual. If a classroom teacher has poor discipline, we teach management methods and monitor the teacher's use of them so the individual teacher can change. If an individual lives in poverty, we offer the person job training skills. This focus on the individual actually perpetuates the status quo, allowing us to deny class division, and circumstances of power created in society and fostering inequity.

The construction of the individual has been the vehicle through which the field of psychology has not only survived but gained power. Lichtman (1987) points out that as capitalism has separated people from social ties, the psychological individual has emerged. In another context, the notion of individual or the field of psychology might not have survived. Psychologists have constructed a language of justification for both the field and the construction of the individual. Solitary beings are characterized as containing psychological traits, personality, sins, abilities, attitudes, and beliefs. Individuals are tested, diagnosed, remediated, treated and sometimes saved. Through the discourse of the individual, those human beings in the field of psychology have generated a deterministic power over both younger and older members of society.

Universal Child Truth

The origins of the belief in universal truth regarding both child and adult can be found in early beliefs in natural law, in universal rules of nature. Combined with the positivist belief in objective reality and scientific discovery, the stage was set for the revelation of universal laws, the truths concerning human beings. As these truths have been constructed most often through psychology and developmental psychology, we have learned to speak of them as if laying bare the true nature and reality of the child. We teach courses in human growth and development as if we know what there is to know about other human beings. We function as if the questions have been answered; and we attempt to create children who fit within those answers.

Hidden/disqualified knowledge. Universalization reifies the group that has been identified, abstracting complex and ambiguous human functioning into simple deterministic entities. For example, psychology and developmental psychology have created domains of development; social, emotional, language, cognitive, physical, moral. Younger human beings, and sometimes older people also, are reduced to listings of functions or stages within particular domains. Besides imposing a predetermined knowledge on "Others," this categorization oversimplifies the knowledge of those Others. Since this oversimplified knowledge does not fit within predetermined categories, it is never recognized, or if revealed is considered irrelevant. For example, a child who denies self-concept because his/her knowledge constructs the earth, nature, and human beings as one, will be accepted as following unusual cultural beliefs but still judged as developing an individual self–concept. In the creation of the universalized, domain–partitioned human being, we limit our ability to create and see the diversity of mankind (Kessen, 1993). Additionally, those who most often apply this universalist notion, such as psychologists and educators, have ignored the political grounding from which psychological domains have emerged. To illustrate, Freud's construction of personality development actually mirrors the obsession with sexuality of the Victorian church and medical community (Foucault, 1978; Ingleby, 1987). Most psychological domain theories have actually reproduced the dominant discourse of the period.

Power production. Psychologists have taken up the notion of universal child truth (and also human truth) and created a science that would reveal predetermined reality. This "claim" to the understanding of children allows experts like psychologists and sometimes educators to construct and maintain control over children, parents and other educators. A judgmental surveillance of these populations is even justified (Burman, 1994; Walkerdine, 1984). A language of normality and pathology is generated within the larger universalist discourse. Younger human beings are labeled as normal or abnormal, as gifted or slow, as mentally healthy or diseased, as competent or inept. The power is created that supports intervention into the lives of others. There is no recognition that without the creation of the concept of normal, abnormal would not exist. Within this context, some are always considered slow, pathological or in some manner lacking and are consequently placed by others into the margins of society. This power is subtle, hidden within attempts to help other human beings to improve their lives, and serves to legitimate the social regulation of groups of human beings, in our case children. The construction of universal child truth or reality creates a power position for adults, and especially psychologists, educators, and other "experts," that sanctions judgment, control, manipulation, correction, and regulation of those who are identified as children.

Challenging the Existence of Childhood

We may or may not choose to believe that "childhood" is a uniquely separate period in the life of human beings. However, we must admit that the creation of childhood is grounded by cultural bias that places limitations on younger human beings and actually lessens the connections that we make with them and each other. Childhood discourses actually conceal and even disqualify certain forms of knowledge, generating power for particular groups and subjugating others. These discourses have not always benefited those who are younger. How can we ignore challenges to the construction of child:

(1)   Historical research and investigations in diverse cultures reveals that human beings are constructed in a variety of ways in a variety of contexts. Younger human beings display remarkable skills and take on major responsibilities in some contexts; they are allowed to play, labeled incompetent, and kept protected from the outside world in others. A "child" in one context is not necessarily a "child" in another.

(2)   The child has been created as a universal truth from within enlightenment/modernist perspectives that focus on scientific reason, dichotomous language and thought, and progress for both the individual and humankind. These positivist beliefs foster the assumptions that there are truths that apply to all human beings and that these truths can be revealed through science. What about people who do not share these beliefs? who do not accept the notion of universal truth? or who would not separate younger human beings from those who are older?

(3)   The construction of childhood as separate from adulthood has varied historically and been most often influenced by those with power. The creation of schools by the clergy to control and protect younger human beings was most likely the defining point for western childhood.

(4)   In western art and literature, younger human beings were used to represent artistic response to societal change. Whether the artist believed in the soul of man or felt helpless and innocent, the child signified these emotions on canvas or in the characters created in literature. The child may have been used simply because he or she was a small human representation. Artists did not necessarily intend to realistically represent the life of younger human beings.

(5)   Science has constructed childhood as the perfect specimen for the scientific gaze. Identification and control of particular populations is accomplished through children.

(6)   Childhood has been/is created through a discourse of adult/child separation. This dichotomy denies knowledge(s) that are constructed and possessed by those who are younger. The concept privileges adult knowledge as what the child will eventually learn and places children in the position to be controlled. We must only expose them to what we have deemed appropriate. Younger human beings are further silenced by the creation of an adult/child dichotomy.

(7)   The construction of child supports the status quo and perpetuates the colonialist power perspective. Younger human beings and their needs are used to deny the political, judicial, economic, and social conditions of society that lead to such circumstances as poverty, ill health, and labeling people as uneducated, lazy, or illiterate. Adults, and most often those adults with money and education, are placed in power.

(8)   Focusing on the individual child as the social unit masks gender, class, and cultural knowledge, denying knowledges that are created as part of groups, cultures, families, and even with peers. Additionally, emphasis on the individual creates the child as ahistorical, asocial, and responsible for the conditions of society.

(9)   The construction of childhood actually reifies younger human beings into simple predetermined entities, denying their human complexities and ambiguities.

(10) A universal child discourse generates positions of power for adults, especially parent over child and psychologist/expert over child, parents, and teachers. The manipulation and regulation of children is legitimized.

Early childhood educators may label these challenges as negative, critiques that are unnecessary and could lead to more problems for children. Some of us would characterize childhood as a positive construct that has lead to the recognition of younger people as human beings who should be valued and respected. After all, conditions of life have improved for some. Children have been removed from factory work; they have been removed from abusive homes; some come to school happy and healthy. Without the concept of child, we would not have constructed the field of early childhood education.

Others of us would propose that at the very least the concept of child requires continual critique, and possibly rejection. Historical problematization reveals a construct that has actually placed a group of people in the position in which others always speak for them. As examples, the reason children do not vote is because we have constructed them as incapable of making the decision (and further allowed them to have no power to obtain that vote). Children are given court advocates because they cannot speak for themselves. Parents make decisions for children. Teachers and psychologists decide what they are capable of, what knowledge is appropriate, and how their behavior should be controlled. With the exception of a few voices of resistance, we do not hear them. We have either silenced them all together or not allowed them to speak unless their voices were consistent with our universalist perspective of children.

Childhood can be interpreted as a positivist construction that has disempowered younger human beings by creating them as incompetent and dependent on adults for care, knowledge, and even bodily control. The discourses of childhood have fostered regulation of a particular group of human beings by another group (described as adults) and generated multiple sites of power for those adults. Additionally, the construction of childhood has not been limited to the universalist view of individual children as the opposite from adults. Childhood is also constructed as a time of progressive development, fostered through idealized forms of early life experience that determine the success and happiness of the individual. Consistent with positivist views of the world as scientifically discoverable truth, the truth for childhood has been grounded in the belief in universal human development and predetermined environmental experience. As we further deconstruct the notion of childhood as a universal human condition, Chapters 3 and 4 are used to critique these assumptions.

Chapter III

Our Allegiance to Child Development

The investment in portraying development as progress works to deny our histories of the personal costs in 'growing up' … turning the complex disorder of individual development into orderly steps to maturity reflects … interests in maintaining social control.

Burman, 1994, p. 19

The discourse of child development has dominated not only the oral communications of those who are concerned for children, but also our professional publications, the research organizations that we have constructed, and the advice that we give to parents and teachers regarding their children. We take action in the name of child development. We propose that schooling be designed around child development. We create research agendas, university classes, and practical materials for the lay public. Our construction of the "child" is dominated by the belief in child development and what the field reveals about younger members of society. Progressive child development is considered foundational, the knowledge base that most appropriately reveals the life worlds of children. This knowledge is used to determine if children are ready to be exposed to particular content and experiences, mature enough to deal with the world around them. We judge the quality of reasoning skill, the social competence, and the physical ability of others based on this knowledge of child development. We have become so involved in this discourse that we assume human development represents the truth for all of us, and especially development as applied to children.

Most of us have stood before others defending the belief that all children progressively develop toward particular adult competencies, skills, and understandings. We have functioned as a field as if all children would be "better off" if their parents and teachers understood child development. We have not questioned development as a socially constructed notion, embedded within a particular historical context and emerging from a distinctive political and cultural atmosphere, and based on a specific set of values. We have not questioned what we think we know about human growth and development, and specifically what we know about children. We have not listened to the voices of children and their families to uncover the influence of our benevolent discourse on them, or whether they agree with this discourse. We have, in fact, assumed that the language of child development represents Truth and benefits all children, from whatever culture, socioeconomic background, or historical period. If others would just view children from a child development perspective, children would always profit.

Our intentions are commendable; we value younger human beings and honestly want their lives to be fulfilled and happy. We have hoped that child development provides an avenue that would promote life for everyone, yet this dream has not been closely examined by the majority of us in the field. We have not asked and pursued critical questions:

Does this discourse actually promote the values that we hold for all human beings?

Do we know what these values are?

If child development is to be our standard, should we not be required to examine this standard with a fine tooth comb?

What are the philosophical assumptions underlying the construction of child development?

What are the hidden messages within these assumptions, the unseen meanings that mold our constructions of the child?

What forms of power and authority are created through the lived text that is child development?

Who is privileged and who is silenced? Are there winners? Are there losers?

Does the discourse of child development actually result in life for all human beings?

The major purpose of this chapter is to reveal the hidden assumptions underlying the notion of child development, to interrupt the official developmental text. This deconstructive process will expose the unconscious cultural values that create the belief in child development, privilege particular ways of knowing, and actually limit possibilities for younger members of society.

The Foundational Assumptions of
Child Development

As a category of developmental psychology that is specifically applied to younger human beings, child development shares in the assumptions that have dominated the field. The first assumption is the belief in human progress, the belief that humanity, groups of humans, and even individual people continually move toward a state that is more advanced. The notion of progress is so common in our every day lives that we do not question it as reality. The second assumption underlying child development is the conviction that all human beings grow and development in a predetermined manner. This belief accepts and includes progress as a natural human state. Finally, the acceptance of the notion of child development assumes a universal human Truth that can be uncovered and applied to all. This universal explanation would ultimately reveal our origins and our destination in life.

The Illusion of Progress

The belief in, or perhaps the illusion of, progress is evident in the conversations of our everyday lives. "Science will one day solve all our problems." "The world is advancing faster than I can keep up with it." "Children have more to learn today than ever before." "She's young; she'll learn more about what people are like." "He doesn't use adult logic, but I see his thinking growing every day." We have constructed the concept of progress as a human given, so accepted in our daily world that it is not questioned. When progress does not appear to have occurred, we conclude that something is wrong. Something is not normal. Yet, historical examination of progress as a concept reveals a grounding in both enlightenment and modernist allegiances to reason. All human cultures have not created progress as a universal. Not only is this history important as it has impacted the construction of the notion of child development, but the ideas are somewhat parallel.

Historical constructions. Bury (1932) has described progress as the idea that human beings are and will continue to move in a desirable direction, that humanity is predetermined to advance. The concept includes the past, present, and future and has over time been expanded to include not only the achievements of humanity, but both individual achievement and predetermined natural change.

The notion of progress was not part of Greek culture, even regarding increased knowledge. For example, Seneca (a member of the Stoic school of philosophy) declared that knowledge would increase and would be used to solve problems. This increased knowledge was not, however, associated with improvement of life as is so common in the Modern Age. Social order represented the ideal for Greek society, with deviation a sign of deterioration. The totally unified world, including "mankind," was viewed as mortal, facing a final, inevitable degeneration. The Greeks were therefore generally prejudiced against change, believing that the salvation of society came from the preservation of already established institutions. Human beings were considered already resourceful enough to handle anything. There was no conceptualization or need for progress.

Early Christians proposed an ultimate happiness for particular human beings in another world. Yet this medieval Christian spirit also excluded the concept of progress or any form of human development. Divine providence meant that the world could end at any time and only a small portion of humanity would lay claim to the happiness offered by another world. The early Christians did embrace the Greek universalist, unified conception of "mankind" that later became an element in the construction of the idea of progress, but they expressed no belief in advancement for all mankind.

As mentioned in the previous chapter, philosophers and thinkers of the fourteenth through seventeenth centuries rejected the dark ghosts of the Middle Ages. This dismissal resulted in the analysis of the work of ancient writers. Although ancient work did not construct progress as a value, decisions to examine the work of the past constructed an atmosphere that would facilitate the notion of progress. Looking at ancient work actually created the belief that the examination of the past could be beneficial. This combination of the past with the present was the beginning of the construction of progress.

Rejecting the degeneration of the world or man, the French historian Jean Bodin reasoned that nature was always uniform. Grounded in the newly emerging beliefs in natural law and reason, he posited a general form of human progress. He believed that the work of the ancients should be commended. However, the progress of modern man was believed to be increasingly evident in more discoveries and greater contributions to thinking. Consistent with the emerging faith in science, Francis Bacon expanded Bodin's ideas by proposing that experimentation could reveal the progressive secrets of nature.

Although Descartes (Chapter 2) ignored the past as if entirely unimportant, and therefore never addressed progress as a construct, the Cartesian spirit that focused on the supremacy of reason and nature shaped the conceptualization of progress. Bernard Fontenelle also advanced the notion, arguing that the intellect of mankind does not degenerate. Fontenelle used Cartesian proof to demonstrate that just as trees in nature have not degenerated, the brain of man has not degenerated. He included the future with the past/present construction of progress and proposed that human intellectual progress is certain and necessary. The course of science and intellectual thought was believed to be in a forward direction independent of particular individual contributions. In a sense, the notion of progress emerged in reaction to the ancient Greek notion of degeneration. Historically, the question could be asked: would progress have been conceptualized if the Greeks had not conceived of the world and mankind as degenerating?

Until the 1700s, progress was related to scientific advance, human intellect and reason. Human emotion and will were considered static. With the publication of *Observations on the Continuous Progress of Universal Reason*, Abbe De Saint-Pierre proposed a view of humanity as also progressing toward human happiness. He believed that both humanity and individual persons moved toward happiness, with the exception that individuals face the loss of both reason and happiness with the onset of feeblemindedness. He further proposed that progress toward the happiness of humanity was slow because of wars, superstition, and rulers who feared the loss of power. St. Pierre believed that progress had accelerated during the time of Bodin and Bacon because greater leisure created avenues for increased exploration. He speculated that the 30 most intelligent children in modern London or Paris would exhibit greater intelligence than the 30 most intelligent children in Constantinople because of the progress achieved in western Europe. Both the time period and the context created difference. He also posited two forms of progress: speculative or scientific, logical advance, and practical or moral advance. Speculative progress was considered more rapid than moral advance. Ethical, political, moral progress required more attention.

Voltaire took up this belief in progress, explaining that the problems of man would disappear as the progressive philosophy became universally accepted. The concept of progress thus became a universalist notion, not simply associated with reason, but accepted as Truth, with application for all humanity.

Bury (1932) has described this period of exploration into the notion of progress as a first phase. French investigators initiated a second phase in which universal progress was accepted as a given and the focus of research was to find laws explaining the progress of civilization. As with Newton in the physical sciences, laws were pursued that could explain the moral world. The science of sociology emerged. For example, August Comte proposed psychological laws of progress, hypothesizing that humanity passed through particular stages in the understanding of each branch of knowledge. The first stage was animistic or theological, yielding authority to a higher power. In the second metaphysical stage, human beings interpreted knowledge through abstraction. In the final stage, humanity used the scientific method to accurately reveal the laws of nature. This positive, scientific stage was the most advanced and led to the understanding of Truths that apply to all human beings. Comte believed that different branches of knowledge were at different stages in development. Although his ideas were not fully accepted, they served as the foundation for sociology and impressed writers such as John Stuart Mill, who went on to describe rules for the investigation of Truth in various fields of knowledge.

At the beginning of the nineteenth century, the work of the French zoologist Jean-Baptiste de Lamarck fostered the notion that the animal kingdom follows particular directional laws of progress. Recapitulation was proposed as an example directional law of animal progress. The first fundamental claim of recapitulation as a law was that there are unitary laws of animal *development*, an ordered sequence of states in a hierarchy. Development was thus introduced as a construct. More specific claims of recapitulation, actually proposed by later followers of Lamarck like Ernst Haeckel and applied to human beings, included the notion that ontogeny recapitulates phylogeny; individual development follows the stages of ancestral development (Morss, 1990).

By the late 1800s, the material progress displayed in the United States and Europe in everyday conveniences resulted in progress as a regular topic of street corner conversation. Darwin's publication of *Origin of Species* in 1859 provided the definitive event in the construction of the concept of progress as an absolute. The third phase in the construction of progress was initiated, the belief in the predetermined progress of mankind. "We may look with some confidence to a secure future of great length ... for the good of each being, all corporeal and mental endowments will tend to progress towards perfection" (Darwin, 1979, p. 223).

Human progress. Darwin's message of evolution suggested humble beginnings to Western man, dethroning him from his position as lord of the reasoning earth. This challenge to man as ruler served to fully establish the idea of progress. A humble pedigree must have meant that man was progressively improving; otherwise why would there be so many material advances? Although evolution has been interpreted in multiple ways, Darwin chose this optimistic view. He even hypothesized that laws of evolutionary progress could be found in areas that had not been previously explored.

Herbert Spencer, Darwin's contemporary, described this connection between evolution and progress in his discussions of sociology and ethics. Human nature was viewed as complex and ever growing. He compared the Newtons and Shakespeares of the world with "houseless savages" (Bury, 1932, p. 337), believing that this contrast proved the progressive variability of human nature. He further proposed that evil is the result of nonadaptation by the organism. Man moves both physically and mentally toward adaptation, ultimately progressing under favorable conditions. Spencer believed that human nature progressively and continuously changes, authoring the phrase "survival of the fittest" (Morss, 1990, p.19). His writings on biology, psychology, and sociology indoctrinated the fields with the concept of progress as Truth for all human beings.

Progress emerged as a linear construct, most often dominated by the western belief in science and reason. Those who constructed the idea were generally White, European males who privileged themselves over those who lived in the past. These individuals lived in a context in which the search for knowledge dominated; science was believed to lead to this ultimate Truth. Science was seen as providing both the evidence for progress and the final revelations as to the natural progress of nature and mankind. Contradictions to linear progress (e.g., war, scientific injury, individual behavior, the irrational) were either ignored or rationalized into nonexistence.

Progress implies a predetermined direction for humanity and individuals and establishes moving forward as a standard for "normalcy." Moving forward is generally defined through the scientific gaze, the gaze of logical thinkers who believe in hierarchy and advancement. Progress implies stable laws of nature that can be applied to all beings in all contexts. The construction of the concept of progress arose from and promoted the belief in determinism, hierarchy, western thought, and universal truth (Mazrui, 1996).

The Belief in Human Development

Development, an ordered sequence of states in a hierarchy, obviously emerged in concert with the construction of the idea of progress. The belief that human beings pass through particular states, and that these stages of change are rooted in human nature (Lichtman, 1987) can also be traced to the Lamarckian focus on recapitulation and to the evolutionist thought of the nineteenth and twentieth centuries. These perspectives have been explored and constructed as science in the field of developmental psychology. More than any other, this field has espoused growth and development as the human condition and created the assumptions that have permeated child development. As with the idea of progress, determinism, hierarchy, and universalism dominate developmental psychology. Further, critiques of dominant domains of developmental research reveal orientations that privilege particular forms of knowledge and create an environment in which particular groups of human beings are positioned to control others.

Developmental psychology. Generally, developmental psychology emerged alongside the field of experimental psychology, not really in a subordinate relationship to it. Both were, however, created within the context of scientific positivism (Morss, 1990). More than any other field, the beliefs and language of developmental psychology have become part of our daily lives, a part of what we expect from ourselves and others (Burman, 1994). We have learned to use developmental terminology, describing ourselves and others as slow, advanced, mature, weak in a particular domain, or ready for a particular experience. We discuss individuals and groups in terms of both ages and stages, explaining behavior based on developmental stage, lack of maturity, or experiences in relation to progress. This discourse has so dominated our own experiences that the perspective is taken for granted. We are not aware of the values contained within the dialogue or that all human beings do not share these values.

Most developmental psychologists describe their field as a subdiscipline in which discoveries are made that contribute to the understanding of human beings. Objective observations and measurements are conducted of human age-related change. The discipline's commitment to rigor is believed to guarantee accuracy in discovery and ethical neutrality. The field is believed to be independent of politics or political purposes because scientific investigation is designed to explore natural human reality, the Truth for human beings (Broughton, 1987).

Burman (1994) describes the emergence of developmental psychology in the late nineteenth century. The quest to find the origins of knowledge led believers in recapitulation (ordered states of development) to study both infants and the adults who were considered "primitives" (those of the "Third" world and those of "color"). Because of their lack of experience, infants were considered savage, undeveloped, and closer to nature. "Primitives" were seen as intellectually less advanced, immature, and, of course, savage. Darwin's child study, in the form of a diary, was accepted as the direction for the examination of infants. Child study emerged as an avenue in the search for the origins of knowledge in concert with European imperialism which also supported anthropological studies of "primitives" in the search for knowledge. These studies of colonized peoples were used to maintain the European belief in racial superiority and to justify imperialist actions. Further, nonstandard behaviors of both children and "primitives" were seen as potentially relevant for the understanding of the newly defined pathological behavior in adults (Foucault, 1965).

The major focus of the child study movement was to observe children in a detached, rational, objective manner. Fathers were viewed as more capable of pursuing such scientific endeavors because of the natural sentimentality of mothers. Women were viewed as incapable of conducting the appropriate objective analysis. "She rather dislikes their being made objects of cold intellectual scrutiny" (Sully, 1881; quoted in Riley, 1983, p. 49). Although child study gave way to developmental psychology and is often discredited within the field, Burman (1994) points to five ways in which the movement impacted further work: (1) belief in investigating the mind; (2) revelations from the minds of children that would lead to understanding adult knowledge; (3) the biologically determined development of the mind; (4) involvement in practices of education and welfare; and (5) institutionalization of the dichotomy between mind and emotion, as illustrated in the belief that males can more appropriately conduct scientific research.

In the late nineteenth century, the upper class of Europe became increasingly concerned with the quality of the population as slums and poor health conditions developed in the newly industrialized cities. Further, the poor populations appeared to be growing at a faster rate than those with more education and money, leading to fears that the middle and upper classes would be contaminated and potentially eliminated. The feebleminded became the "object of political anxiety and scientific intervention" (Burman, 1994, p. 13). Concerned about the effects of environmental conditions, Francis Galton constructed the nature/nurture question that has grounded research in psychology since that time. By 1880, both England and France had established compulsory elementary education to ward off poverty, viewed as a human trait rather than a set of social circumstances (Hendrick, 1990; Rose, 1990; Walkerdine, 1984). In addition to concern for the origins of knowledge, a concern for regulating those individuals who might be out of societal control emerged. Simultaneously, the child and the poor or deviant individual were created as objects of science to be observed, understood, and controlled (Burman, 1994).

The mathematical domination of scientific reason created an environment in which all forms of psychology, including development, were considered measurable. Gould (1981) has traced the reification of intelligence as measurable first by the size of the head, then through body measurement, and finally through a numbered testing scale. Galton, who was highly respected during the period, believed that with enough ingenuity, anything could be measured. This belief in measurement provided the tool for regulation of those who were feared, those who did not conform, or those who were not understood.

Human development was constructed as a natural, and therefore universal, unchangeable, Truth in two ways. First, mental testing in the form of IQ measurement and its association with chronological age led to the creation of quantifiable scales. This scaling supported the work of Arnold Gesell in the United States who placed scores of children under surveillance and described stages of development associated with ages. Secondly, the mental was incorporated with the medical. The faith in reason was incorporated into the already existing authority of medicine (Burman, 1994; Harris, 1987), creating a belief in the human being as biological and governed by natural scientific law. Medicine, combined with the illusion of Truth created by statistical norming, constructed human development as a universal that predicted and described all human life.

The construction of stages can be traced to a variety of sources that include literature and social activity as well as such ideas as ancient as the Greek belief in the number 7. The Greeks considered age 7 to be the age of reason, 14 to be adolescence, and 21 to represent maturity. (Remember that the Greeks did not believe in progress. They believed in the number 7.) *oh!* During the Depression in the United States, the age 65 was chosen as a retirement age. Human developmental characteristics related to aging were not the source of the decision. The largest number of people would be removed from a swollen work force by using the age 65. Further, Piaget's stages correspond to the time spent with family and in schooling that already existed in Europe before his theories were developed (Lichtman, 1987). Add the Lamarkian notion of development as ordered states in a hierarchy and stages are generated.

Developmental psychology emerged as a discipline philosophically committed to science, truth, and objectivity, "a paradigmatically modern" field (Burman, 1994, p. 157). "Developmental psychology classifies, orders, and coordinates the phases of our growth and even defines what is and is not to be taken as growth" (Broughton, 1987, p. 1). The surveillance, measurement, judgment, and comparison of children (and other human beings) creates the conditions for social control, man over woman, adult over child, middle class over the poor. In "The Difficulty of Being a Child in French–Speaking Countries," Voneche (1987) illustrates how the direction of progress in the field has not even attempted to attend to the actual person but rather has attended to social control. Binet's two daughters, Piaget's three children, and the "wild child" Victor are some of the children who are presented. "When Victor came out of the woods, everyone knew what to do with him; catch him and normalize him" (p. 62). The first concern of the state was to liberate him by teaching what was "appropriate" for human beings. "Nobody cared to know more about his life in the woods of Aveyron. No one went along with him"(p. 63).

Specific critiques. As Broughton (1987) points out, the construction of bodies of knowledge represents the advocacy of particular values, of specific desired outcomes. Without recognition of the values that construct them, these knowledges are presented as discovered through the use of objective, scientific investigation. An illusion of truth is created. Through this illusion, we have not only been convinced that development is a truth for all human beings, but that we can categorize and describe various types of development; cognitive, language, social, and so on (Durkheim & Mauss, 1963). The following are brief critiques of two of the child development knowledge bases, infant development and Piagetian cognitive development.

Questions regarding infant development have always been grounded in the underlying modernist search for the origins of knowledge within the individual. Based on the assumption that knowledge is discoverable, social and cultural context and indeterminate or ambiguous human behaviors are ignored. Burman illustrates this pervasive bias in the the construction of infant development research by analyzing the visual cliff study conducted by Gibson and Walk (1960; 1973). Creating a visual cliff covered by thick glass, the researchers claimed that infants demonstrated depth discrimination by refusing to crawl over the glass to their mothers. Burman points out that the study, considered a classic that is repeatedly described in developmental psychology texts (e.g., Dworetsky, 1990; Kaplan, 1991; Mitchell, 1992), is not even recognized as a social situation. The social embeddedness of the laboratory test, the materials used, the facial expression of the mothers, the fact that mothers were used as the child's motivational object, are reduced to the singular issue of individual development. Further, why was depth perception chosen over the complex social understanding of human communication illustrated by the infant and mother?

Much developmental literature addresses the difficulty in interpreting infant behavior. Yet we might observe these same difficulties with 4–year–olds, 14–year–olds, or 44–year–olds. Perhaps this difficulty applies to all human behavior and our attempts to interpret that behavior, or even in the belief that behavior reveals the human being. Perhaps the difficulty is actually embedded in the notion of progressive development, in the belief that there exists a human developmental Truth and that we can interpret that Truth.

The commitment to scientific truth, objectivity, and reason is well illustrated in Piaget's description of the child as a developing scientist, systematically examining problems in the real world, hypothesizing, and learning how to solve the problems through discovery (Burman, 1994; Piaget, 1957). An uphill model of human change (similar to that of scientific discovery and European veiws of cultural progress) is posited

(Rorty, 1980), in addition to a hierarchical model of cognitive structures. While the model includes the notion of individual construction, the developmental path, the way of knowing, and the content to be known are considered common to all regardless of culture or life history. Children (and peoples who represent societies that are not grounded in European cultural values) are represented as less advanced (or more primitive) and are by implication placed in the political and social margin (Cleverly & Phillips, 1986; Gould, 1981), — that is, in positions from which they are controlled.

In multiple ways, Piaget's theories reinforced the dominant beliefs of his time. For example, the mental was privileged over the active, contributing to the thinking versus doing dichotomy, the abstract versus the concrete. When knowledge is described as progressively more adequately organized, adult is privileged over child, rationality over irrationality. The concept of autonomy is actually imperialist in that some cultures do not value individualistic models of humanity. Further, the focus on the autonomous individual can result in the denial of racial, class, gender, and cultural inequities (Buck-Morss, 1975; Sullivan, 1974). Voneche (1987) also points to Piaget's belief in the ultimate childhood innocence by asking the child "What do you think?," as if the child would respond independently of culture, context, or the power relationship present in the interview situation.

Walkerdine (1988) points out that Piaget's work further displays his commitment to the elimination of war and the triumph of reason over emotion. His discourse of logical reason and autonomy reflect his belief in a rational, democratic society, not in a naturally occurring human condition. Walkerdine places Piaget in his own cultural context; his values led to the construction of an egocentric and ethnocentric illusion of truth, the illusion that all human beings progress through logical development as perceived by Piaget.

Recent events in developmental psychology have perpetuated the same developmental perspective that led to surveillance and control. For example, the construction of the field of adult development and education legitimizes further control of a disenfranchised population and the construction of schooling devices to regulate them (Broughton, 1987). Illiterate is constructed and defined as characterizing a particular group and requiring a solution. Illiterate adults are then blamed for the ills of society and regulated through testing, categorization, and further education (Rockhill, 1993).

Universal Truth

The belief in child development represents the conviction that there are particular truths, determined even before a person's life begins, that apply to all human beings. These truths dominate whether one lives in Africa, Australia, or the United States, in a busy city, on a farm, or in a war–torn slum, in the twentieth century or two thousand years ago. The origins of the belief in universal truth are discussed in Chapter 2 as associated with the construction of the belief in natural law, in universal rules of nature. The enlightenment belief that science would reveal the true laws of nature, the way the system functions, is well illustrated in the construction of child development. The modern belief in progress and development have combined with this universalist notion to create the description of the human child. This child explores the world as a scientist as he or she passes through predetermined stages of change in various areas of growth (e.g., linguistic, cognitive, social, emotional, moral, physical) toward the competent, autonomous adult model. Our belief in universals, progress, and hierarchical change have been scientifically "discovered" in the child. We have accepted these discoveries as true for everyone.

Through this western perspective, developmental psychology has "globalized childhood" (Boyden, 1990). We have convinced ourselves that younger human beings are the same all over the world. We have ignored the variation in cultural values, the position of children in various cultures, and the power held by children. For example, in a culture in which younger human beings are viewed as competent and contributing to the family welfare, they are also seen as powerful and equal members of society. Nieuwenhuys (1994) describes this context as she discusses the Indian state of Kerala. Males and females of all ages work together for the survival of the village. Without the involvement of the younger members of the society, the village would not survive. These "children" may actually have more power within their society than the "children" that we have identified as in need of protection. In the 1990s we talk again of the problems with child labor, especially in the so-called Third World. Most of us could agree that no human beings should be placed (and sometimes locked) in sweat shops for 10, 12 or more hours a day with poor lighting, poor ventilation, little food or water, and unsanitary conditions. But this is an issue for all humanity; no human should be placed in these conditions. When we globalize younger human beings and make labor a children's issue, we actually disempower children in particular contexts, as discussed in Chapter 2, and we establish a discourse that supports the notion that younger human beings cannot be powerful. Further, this globalized discourse allows us to ignore the imperialist actions that have led in many cases to poor living and work conditions for human beings of all ages in particular contexts.

As mentioned in the previous chapter, universalizing a particular group of people creates the conditions for social control. Our Euro–American system of psychology and education illustrates this well. Because we believe in universal child development, we feel that we understand children. Allowing for individual variation, we describe what a two–year–old is like, the differences between three– and four–year–olds, what a class of kindergartners will be like, common behavior for preadolescents and adolescents, and on and on. We have come to believe that observation of younger human beings is not only appropriate but necessary. Otherwise we cannot understand them and place them into the appropriate category of growth. Although we espouse flexibility, we have created complete educational curriculums around the "truths" of child development. We have convinced ourselves that child development is a flexible notion because child–centeredness, exploration, and discovery are included. (See the discussion of child–centeredness and play in Chapter 6.) Child development has so globalized younger human beings that we would probably suggest that learning centers, scientific exploration, and language experience fit all children in all educational classrooms all over the world. The belief that child development universally describes children actually denies the multiple realities of children's lives (Silin, 1995). Younger human beings are expected to live within our child development expectations, and they may even respond to these expectations, never revealing their real worlds, the worlds that go beyond what we have conceived.

The Hidden Messages Within
Child Development

Within the construction, assumptions, and practices of child development are cultural messages and actions that lead to social inequity and injustice for younger members of society and even for some of us who are older. However unrecognized, unconscious, or unintended, these messages create an environment that is unjust and even hostile to particular groups of human beings. The messages that I choose to discuss are: (1) the construction of multiple forms of privilege and subjugation within the belief in child development; (2) social regulation as intrinsic within the belief; (3) the creation of a quality hierarchy among human beings; and (4) a deficiency model of humanity.

Privilege and Subjugation

Within the construction of child development are multiple forms of privilege and subjugation. First, the construction of development and the underlying belief in progress is a hierarchical notion. Those who live now are privileged over those who lived in the past. Those who are at higher levels are privileged over those who have not yet reached those levels. Functioning at higher levels even allows one to observe those who are at lower levels as subjects to be studied and judged. Those who have identified the forms of knowledge that are represented in child development — for example logical thought — are privileged over those who would choose knowledge from more diverse locations — as examples, collaborative forms of moral behavior, music, or knowledge based on group solidarity. Piagetian logical thought is considered more important than African constructions of beauty. When certain groups, individuals, or even forms of knowledge are privileged, others are subjugated, placed in the margin of society. This subjugation can be observed in multiple forms: as lacking in credibility or validity, as unimportant, as nonexistent. Within adult constructions of dominant knowledge, the lived worlds of children and the knowledge that they possess are ignored and denied.

Second, a biological hegemony is created over other ways of understanding or perceiving humanity. A normalized vision of the child is produced (Walkerdine, 1988) which again creates privilege for those who fit that vision and places in the margin as deficient, wrong, or abnormal, those who do not fit the vision. Further, when humanity is viewed as biologically predetermined, the unclear, ambiguous aspects of human life are placed in the margin. Resistance, fluid character, unpredictability, complexity, and obscurity are denied.

Finally, this child development construction allows those who are in power, those who are more privileged, to ignore the pain and inequity of others. When human beings are considered as growing and developing, the privileged can rationalize and deny their roles in the construction of the human condition. "Third World peoples have not developed as far as the United States. Give them another 50 or 75 years and they will have the technology and understandings that we have." The role of the privileged in the creation of that privilege is denied and human beings are further subjugated as less well developed.

Social Regulation

Child development is actually a covert method for social control and regulation. The expectations that everyone will or should progress, each individual will exhibit particular behaviors at particular periods in their life, and some human beings function at lower levels than others intrinsically establishes an environment in which certain individuals (or groups) would expect to regulate others. These expectations serve as norms, which are actually disguised as fact, as truth that should be applied to all. Those who do not fit the norms are then guided (read regulated) toward avenues that would lead to the fulfillment of developmental expectations. The concept of maturity is an example of developmental construction used to regulate children every day, a value–laden norm masked as natural fact. Through our continued surveillance, children are judged as mature or not quite ready. They are taught to read or asked to wait, admitted to kindergarten or held in preschool, judged as socially competent or in need of intervention. We have come to believe that a fruit maturing in an orchard without intervention is the same as a young human being learning western logic. This belief structure places those with the western–determined developmental knowledge (most often the educated middle class) in power, and those who do not share or agree with that knowledge in positions to either be controlled or to resist that power.

Developmental psychology, as applied to whatever age group, functions as a tool of cultural imperialism. Cultures that do not agree with or respond to developmental expectations are categorized as backward, as needing to learn from those who are more advanced. This perspective is used to justify both physical and intellectual imperialism.

Human Hierarchy

Child development constructs a perspective of superiority/inferiority. As long as we believe in hierarchies of human beings, some individuals will be placed at the bottom, whether young children or primitive adults, females, or people of color. The norms for the development hierarchy are those that are consistent with the dominant social ideology. Women are an excellent example of those whose ways of knowing the world have not dominated and who have, consequently, been devalued by stage theorists, from Freud to Piaget. Discussed in the previous chapter, Kohlberg's moral stages are an excellent example. Women and cultures that do not value total independence from the social world would never reach the highest stages of moral functioning. Further, women as adults have not even been allowed to be independent. Walkerdine (1988; Walkerdine et al., 1989) discusses child development as a gendered construction, promoting the hegemonic male over female hierarchy. Gendered child development is well illustrated in the advertisement of toys in which the child is represented as the male exploring scientist or the masculine pioneer. The supremacy that we afford to the scientific method and logic in child development privileges a form of cultural masculinity.

Child development places children at the lowest level of the hierarchy, the most inferior. Based on this inferior position, we rationalize our continued surveillance of them. We not only feel that it is appropriate to intervene into the lives of children, but we actually give them no privacy. We teach how to observe children and that it is necessary to observe them. What would happen if we attempted to continuously, and often covertly, observe our colleagues, our bosses, our neighbors, or our adult friends and family members? Most of them would refuse to be under our constant analysis, to be part of our scientific gaze. Most would feel that we were judging them rather than treating them as human beings.

Humanity as Deficient

Human development, and especially child development, provides a view of humanity that is always deficient. Human beings are always progressing through one stage or the other, growing, changing, learning. We are never complete; we have never arrived at what we will become. The child is especially incomplete, only a shadow of his/her future self. Perhaps this belief in the child as becoming actually keeps us from knowing him/her as a human being living with us in the present.

We are always attempting to overcome this deficiency, to learn that which we have not learned, to think in a more advanced way, to learn to understand ourselves better. We have established the belief that every child under quality educational conditions wants to learn. Each of us should want to go as far in school as possible, to pursue more education in multiple ways. This focus on ever–continuing progress and development establishes a context in which many of us will never be satisfied, never feel worthy, never have advanced enough. There is a possibility that one human being is happy with the belief that he/she should always grow and change, but should that belief be imposed on all of humanity? Should individuals have the choices of living in the present, living in the past, or living however they like without pressure to progress imposed by others?

Limiting Possibilities

This deconstruction of child development will, by many, be viewed as inappropriate, as potentially damaging to children. Child development has been the foundation for child advocacy in early education and social welfare, the standard for the care and education of children. We must, however, recognize that this foundation has feet of clay. It does not represent a truth that should be applied to all younger human beings, but a set of beliefs that have been constructed within a particular social, political, cultural, and historical context by a particular group of people with power over other groups of people (e.g., their own children, women, people who are not from Europe or the United States). Assumptions concerning human beings underlie this set of beliefs:

(1) Child development has been constructed based on enlightenment/modernist notions of human progress that are linear, universalist, deterministic, and that establish advancing as a standard for "normalcy." Those who do not fit are abnormal.

(2) Developmental psychology has legitimized the surveillance, measurement, and social control of children and other marginalized groups in the name of normal growth and human change.

(3) Child development theories have fostered dominant ideologies and created privilege for those in power. Examples include the establishment of hierarchical stages and the privileging of logical thought.

(4)   Child development is an imperialist notion that justifies categorizing children and diverse cultures as backward, needing help from those who are more advanced.

(5)   Child development places younger human beings in the least powerful position, always at the lowest level of the hierarchy, the most inferior.

(6)   The construction of child (and human) development assumes human deficiency. The child is always becoming, always attempting to learn something new, to advance, to become an adult. (Even adults can never be satisfied because they must always be developing.)

If we choose to construct the child and to use child development as part of that construction, we should minimally recognize the beliefs that underlie notions of development and who is empowered and disempowered by those beliefs. More importantly, we should recognize that younger human beings have played no role in the construction of childhood or in the creation of child development as the dominant knowledge form. More and more, even those who have dominated the field recognize that child development has emerged from what adults considered worthy of study (See Katz, 1996; Lubeck, 1996; Stott & Bowman, 1996). Living within our values, younger human beings are limited to the possibilities that fit our constructions of them.

Chapter IV

Using Early Experience to Judge Mother and Family

Morality was systematically linked to the economic factor, involving a continuous surveillance of the family, a full penetration into the details of family life.

Donzelot, 1979, p. 69

Recent childhood discourse is dominated by the assumption that early experience in one way or the other determines the life of the individual (Bloom, 1964: Hunt, 1961). This discourse is evidenced in child development and guidance books, displayed in the media, heard in parent conversations, and employed by legislators, child advocates, medical personnel, and education professionals. Psychoanalytic, behaviorist, psychometric, ethological, and Piagetian constructivist developmental psychologies have universally posited this belief (Kessen, 1981). Those of us in early childhood education have accepted the discourse to the extent that we chose to work with younger human beings as our careers. Some of us may not believe that the early years are more important than any other part of a person's life, but we have certainly accepted the notion that early experience is the foundation, if not the determiner, of later life. We have even constructed rules for these early experiences; how they should look and sound, who should be part of the experiences, how often they should occur, and within what context. We have constructed methods for advising parents and teachers of young children as to the why and how of experiences.

In our rush to make the world better for younger human beings, we have not, however, questioned the values underlying the concept of early experience, the ways that a societal focus on the early years conflicts with the lived experiences of various groups of people, or the ways that focusing on early experience may disempower people and even ultimately limit human possibility. Further, the family is perceived as the major provider of early experience. Based on the "quality" of early experience that is provided and ignoring contradictory evidence (Clarke & Clarke, 1976; Rutter, 1981; Tizard, 1991), the family, and especially the mother, has been held responsible for the child's well-being throughout his/her life. Families are expected to provide particular types of early experiences for their children and are judged as deficient, pathological, perhaps even in need of intervention if the child exhibits what society has judged to be problematic behavior. One needs only to examine the current political discourse in the United States to see evidence of how families are tied to the notion of early experience and blamed for everything from school failure to poverty to violence on the streets. We get the message from all sides that the family is responsible. If families would just provide the appropriate early experiences and support for their children, our problems would disappear. Families, and particular family members like mothers, are placed in the position of total responsibility for the conditions of society. Parents are expected to be perfect, performing within a range of behaviors that have been constructed as those that provide appropriate early experiences for children. Otherwise, they are failures, do not love their children, and are judged as less competent human beings.

I would not question the importance of every part of the life of human beings. We all appear to need sustenance and circumstances in which we can thrive. I would question the notion that we could ever know exactly what those circumstances are for everyone. Further, functioning as if we *do* understand those circumstances oversimplifies human life, devalues the diversity with which we are blessed, and places many of us as human beings in "no win" situations and even positions of powerlessness.

The purposes of this chapter are therefore to deconstruct the assumption that early experience determines human life and to examine the gendered, power–oriented environment fostered by dogmatic adherence to the notion. In this case, deconstruction is used as a process of critique to identify the dominant themes surrounding early experience (Burman, 1994). Questions include:

How did the belief in early experience as the definer of later life emerge?
What are the unconscious cultural values underlying this belief?
Are particular ways of viewing the world or specific knowledges privileged by the notion of early experience?
Are particular groups of people advantaged or disadvantaged by the belief?

The Construction of Early Experience

Faith in the importance of early experience so dominates western perspectives, and especially beliefs held in the United States, that providing children with appropriate experiences is considered a moral imperative. This belief has emerged from the enlightenment/modernist context that promoted science as the key to nature and all forms of human life. (See Chapter 2 for a briefing on dominant enlightenment and modern perspectives and Chapter 3 for the continuation of the discussion as applied to human development.) The themes that underlie the notion of early experience are complex and originate from a variety of sources. First is the construction of the "child" as an avenue in the search for the origins of knowledge, the child as reflecting the origins of "adult" reason. Second is the universalist, ahistorical notion of self as created through early interaction with parents, and perpetuated in psychoanalytic theory. The construction of young human beings as equivalent and comparable to young animals is the third theme. The fourth is the creation of the mother/child unit as one human body, meaningless without each other. The final theme, the family as the creator, determiner, and even terminator of the child, is inextricably tied to the first four.

Child as the Origin of Man

The overwhelming belief in early experiences as dominating the future life of the individual emerged from the Western enlightenment and modernist contexts in which science was/is believed to reveal the secret truths of the universe. The belief in the progress of knowledge and reason as exhibited by the adult male lead to the search for the origins of that knowledge. Believers in the Lamarckian focus on recapitulation, or human progress through ordered states of development (see Chapter 3), were directed to the study of both infants and those adults who were considered "primitive" (non–white and non–European). The child and primitive adults represented a lower evolutionary state of man. In this context, the child–study movement emerged dominated by the conviction that children should be rationally and objectively observed and that these detached surveillances would reveal from the mind of the child the origins of adult reason. Although claiming to be science, not child study, developmental psychology is a field with the same convictions, the belief that science can reveal the origins of knowledge and that surveillance, measurement, and analysis of children can unveil that knowledge. Even Piaget, whose work is more recent, focused not on younger human beings but on the construction of knowledge (Burman, 1994). Viewing the child as a vehicle through which knowledge was expected to originate, we could expect that the early years (and early experiences) would gain prominence. The act of studying infants as the evolutionary baseline actually supports the idea that early experience is the determiner of the child's life. This idea was not generated because of importance to the child, but because early experience was constructed as important to the scientific gaze in the search for knowledge.

Additionally, in the newly industrialized cities of Europe in the nineteenth century, the upper class became concerned with the growing population of people living in poverty. Associating poverty with feeblemindedness, they feared that those who were educated and monied would become contaminated and eventually overrun by those who were inferior. Compulsory education was quickly established to provide a control mechanism for those living in poverty. Children were expected to attend school in an attempt to ward off the inferior inherited characteristics that had caused their parents to become poor (Hendrick, 1990; Rose, 1990; Walkerdine, 1984). Again, a belief in early experience surfaced, not because of an intrinsic concern for younger human beings, but as a control mechanism for a population that was feared.

Freud and Early Experience

An understanding of Freudian psychology is crucial in an examination of faith in the importance of early experience (Osborn, 1991; Ruch, 1967). Born in 1856 in Europe, the young Freud was taken with the work of Charles Darwin and later entered medicine because of his belief and interest in human nature. He believed that his own early experiences profoundly impacted his adulthood, citing events that dominated his own memory. The first childhood conflict was considered to be the birth and subsequent death at 8 months of his younger brother. Feeling that he had lost the exclusive love of his mother upon his brother's birth, Freud admitted evil thoughts toward the infant. When the baby died, he blamed himself for the death, the beginning of a form of lifelong criticism. Freud also admitted that as a child he had been sexually aroused by seeing his mother naked. The impact of these events on Freud are evidenced in the creation of his major theories: the role played by childhood conflicts in later life and the theory of infantile sexuality (Jones, 1953-57).

Although Freud was viewed as controversial and even radical for his day, Foucault (1978) has pointed out how his theories actually reproduced the dominant discourses of Victorian Europe. The Victorian church and the medical profession, the powers that dominated late nineteenth and early twentieth century Europe, were obsessed with controlling sexuality, especially in children and women. Freud's theories were actually consistent with the ideology of these dominant views. The construction of early life as entirely grounded in sexual desire creates an expectation for control and repression by the individual and society and the regulation of childhood. Additionally, the construction of naturally occurring stages in personality development reflects the growing belief of the times in scientific determinism, the belief that human life is a predetermined progressive condition that is universal and natural and that can be revealed through science. Finally, Freud applied his own beliefs about himself universally to all human beings. He did not recognize that his ideas were tied to his own historical context or that the beliefs about his own childhood did not necessary apply to all other human beings.

Freud's construction of female experience is tied to the privileging of early experience for males and females. Believing that each little girl feels inferior and wounded because she does not have a penis, he proposed that she contents herself with the knowledge that she will bear a child. The baby substitutes for the penis. Freud viewed motherhood as the only way that a woman could reach sexual fulfillment and psychological maturity (Chodorow, 1978; Eyer, 1992; S. Freud, 1962). Motherhood was the natural state for females and was tied to infancy. Mothers were to do nothing to endanger childbearing and were the architects of the child in the early years. In her ultimate role as mother, the female controlled the balance between childhood pleasure and control. Early experiences with one's mother resulted in an adult who was either adjusted to the demands of civilized society or maladapted (Eyer, 1992). Rather than illustrating the role of early experience in anyone's life, Freudian theory reveals the conviction that males are superior and that women and children must be controlled.

Child–guidance clinics emerged in the early part of the twentieth century in both England and the United States based on the Freudian theory that early relationships with parents, and especially mothers, determined later life. Work in the clinics focused on research and treatment of juvenile delinquency and assumed causal ties to infancy and the early years.

Uncomfortable with Freud s focus on sexuality and the notion of sexual impulses in young children, English and American therapists revised psychodynamic theory. For example, Ian Suttie challenged Freud's total focus on the sexual instinct. In *The Origins of Love and Hate* (1935), Suttie posited that the need for love and companionship is biologically present at birth. The need for love was considered equal in importance to the sexual instinct and also the source of adult pathology. Consistent with Freudian theory, a family member and most often the mother was considered the love object with whom the young child's drives were met. These therapists categorized children as normal or pathological and blamed their mothers as being either too mechanical and cold in dealing with their children or too overprotective. Mothers who did not demonstrate the appropriate balance of love and companionship were at fault (Eyer, 1992). Again, the discourse is early experience, but the hidden message is judging children and their mothers.

Animal Babies

Attempting to understand evolution across a wide variety of species, American psychologists began to study animals in their laboratories in the 1940s and 1950s. Although animal behavior within natural habitats was judged to vary even within a particular species, laboratory–induced normalized animal behavior in the form of a mother/child unity, soon emerged as analogous to human behavior. As examples, goats seem to form bonds with their kids while roe deer often adopt alien fawns, yet fallow deer reject them (Eyer, 1992); most tamarins (a small monkey in South America) abandon their young if care assistance is not available from community members; further, infant cannibalization is not uncommon in mammals, especially as a strategy for survival (Hrdy, 1995). Although scientists were aware of these contradictions, the human mother and child were immediately compared to a normalized construction of animals. This animal comparison resulted in the expectation that a mother/child unity was natural. To function without this unity was considered abnormal and pathological. Women and children were likened to animals — usually animals that were being controlled by researchers.

The most familiar example of this analogy is the work of Harry Harlow (1959) in the 1950s at the University of Wisconsin. After isolating infant rhesus monkeys to keep them free of disease, Harlow found that their behavior differed from those monkeys who were not isolated. Viewing this behavior as abnormal, he began to explore the amount of isolation that infant monkeys could withstand. Concluding from this work that the presence of the mother was necessary for normal behavior and development in the rhesus monkey, he applied his conclusions to all primates. Further, in his work he constructed a variety of mother types using surrogate mothers constructed of cloth or wire. The mother/infant dyad and the impact of early experience were assumed and were summarily applied to human beings. All other relationships and contextual conditions for life were ignored. Haraway (1989) has illustrated the gender bias in Harlows work in the construction of such surrogates as the "cloth mother" and attempts to rear the "evil mother." The use of the term "rape rack" for the instrument used to artificially inseminate female monkeys is perhaps the best example. Additionally, at a time in the United States in which women had been forced back home after working during World War II, he constructed a "nuclear family apparatus," with interlocking cages that illustrated how a family should live. Further, Haraway points out that even if the animal/human comparison were appropriate, the lives of animals used in the research were totally denaturalized. Rhesus monkeys would not under any conditions, natural or otherwise, place themselves in cages to be manipulated.

Using animal/human analogies, the importance of early experience was supported using experiences that were constructed from a simplistic, regulatory perspective. Not only were experiences controlled such that they were not natural and would never occur outside of a laboratory, but the context of the laboratory and the constructed experiences were excluded. For example, some of Harlow's monkeys lived with other infant monkeys. No attention was given to the relationship between the young animals. Others had no animal contact. Tortured animals (e.g., those who were regularly catapulted into the air or beaten with brass spikes) exhibited unusual behaviors which would most likely happen whether the animal was raised by an accepting mother, father, other community member monkey, or alone. Early experience was not the issue; placing particular groups (e.g., animals, women, young children) under the control of those who construct what is considered appropriate was the underlying agenda.

Proper Mothering
During the latter half of the twentieth century, psychological research joined with medicine in the construction of "proper mothering" for human

infants. This proper mothering discourse constructed the belief that young human beings must have a particular, universal set of early experiences to survive. An almost mystical importance was placed on the role of the mother and included the construction of maternal deprivation, attachment, and bonding.

Maternal deprivation. Working in the Tavistock guidance clinic in London, John Bowlby was commissioned by the World Health Organization to report on the conditions of orphaned children in the United States and Europe. He subsequently reviewed a body of medical research published during the previous 20 years on infants. This review revealed that young children who lived in institutions were continually judged as inferior, mentally and emotionally (Bowlby, 1951). Bowlby's conclusions were that these children suffered from lack of relationship with their mothers, a maternal deprivation that could even lead to death (Spitz, 1945). Further, he hypothesized that maternal deprivation could occur not only in institutions like orphanages or hospitals but in a home that outwardly seemed normal. If the mother did not provide the care needed, the child could suffer partial deprivation. Counselors were advised to search out homes in which the mother (or mother substitute) was unconsciously rejecting the young child, was insecure, or exhibited inappropriate condemnation of the child (Eyer, 1992). "Deprived children, whether in their homes or out of them, are a source of social infection as real or serious as are the carriers of diphtheria or typhoid" (Bowlby, 1951, p. 157).

In 1953, he published a version of the 1951 book in a simplified form titled *Child Care and the Growth of Love* that became a best seller in England. Claiming that full-time maternal employment was like the "death of a parent" (Bowlby, 1951, p.73), Bowlby's work focused on keeping mothers at home with their children and was enthusiastically accepted by social workers and eventually supported by physicians (Eyer, 1992). The concept was applied in multiple contexts and situations involving children. For example, in England over 700,000 children had been separated for various reasons from their parents during World War II (van den Berg, 1972). When these children later exhibited problems such as bed–wetting, the maternal deprivation theory was applied. Conditions of war, economy, or society were not considered.

By the mid–1950s, the medical community had accepted the research on maternal deprivation, resulting in a shift from attending solely to the child's physical condition to concern for her/his emotional health. Hospital practices were reformed and young children were being placed in foster care rather than institutions. The term maternal deprivation, although representing a range of conditions from institutionalization and multiple caretaking to newly constructed concepts like neglect, separation, overprotection, and rejection (Eyer, 1992), both produced and exercised power over mothers. Women as mothers were linguistically blamed for all the conditions in which society may have placed its young members, from isolation in orphanage cubicles with little human contact to exposure to medical epidemics.

Attachment. Furthering his belief in the mother/infant unit, Bowlby constructed a theory of attachment, the child's continuous warm relationship with his/her mother. He hypothesized that the infant instinctually attaches to the mother, creating a primary social bond. This instinctual need was felt to exist for both animals and humans and would result in developmental disaster if not met (Bowlby, 1958). Working with Ugandan infants, Mary Ainsworth (1967) furthered the notion by proposing three attachment types; secure, insecure, and unattached (avoidant). This work led to attempts to document the development of attachment behaviors including the age that the young child appeared attached to basically one person and the age that the child could deal with strangers (Schaffer & Emerson, 1964).

In the 1970s mother/infant research accelerated. Mother/infant dyads were audiotaped, videotaped, and otherwise placed under surveillance. Yet, much of the work on both maternal deprivation and attachment was contradicted. To illustrate, research with diverse cultural groups called to question the existence of a sensitive period for development or of primary attachment (Reed & Leiderman, 1983). Working mothers and their children did not experience attachment difficulties (Kagan, Kearsly, & Zelazo, 1978). The theoretical perspective was also questioned. For example, Kagan proposed that children who may be labeled as avoidant may not need to be as close to their mothers because of individual differences in constitutional make–up. Some people may naturally need less proximity to others. Additionally, by decontextualizing emotion and adult/child relationship, Ainsworth placed undue emphasis on the issue of mother–child separation, excluding the larger social contexts in which the child exists both from daily and overall perspectives (Leavitt, 1994).

Finally, critical analysis reveals that the concept of attachment fosters dominant gender perspectives as well as notions of class and cultural privilege. Living within a construction such as attachment, the child is expected to move from the stereotypic feminine "attachment" to the culturally determined masculine "detachment" (Burman, 1994). Maturity has become "the masculine capacity to tolerate separation" (p. 87). The mother is held responsible for the process and must ultimately reject the child for the achievement of the independence of autonomy. The concept fosters patriarchy and creates women as the inferior beings who are held responsible for the perpetuation of their own oppression. Additionally, little girls are expected to both exhibit detachment and to remain attached to the forms of patriarchy that will control their lives (Broughton, 1987; Walkerdine, 1988). This perspective further assumes that mothers have the economic flexibility to respond to these directives and the cultural inclination to be regulated by gendered expectations.

Although both research and theoretical criticism abounds, attachment continues to play a major role in the construction of the belief in particular types of early experience. Mothers and infants, with the minimalized addition of fathers and family members, remain the topic of research, surveillance, and even popular culture and street corner discussions. We have accepted the mother/infant dyad without questioning the isolation that is created around them. We have rendered their separate identities as meaningless and their relationships to others and the societal context as nonexistent or unimportant.

Bonding. In the 1970s, Marshall Klaus and John Kennell (1976) reported that mothers placed with their infants for extensive hours immediately following birth displayed better mothering skills and their infants displayed more advanced development than those without the extensive contact. They explained their findings by proposing a hormonally determined sensitive period immediately following birth in which mothers are primed to accept or reject their infants, to bond with the child. Kennell and Klaus toured the country conducting workshops on bonding. By the 1980s, their research had been dismissed by the scientific community as poorly conceived and inaccurate, but physicians and nurses embraced the idea, providing special rooms for bonding in hospitals. Multiple organizations popularized the idea, from fundamentalist religious groups to natural child birth organizations to the mass media. Even some feminists, who stood for women's rights to be employed, saw bonding as a way to insure the child's psychological health early on so that women felt comfortable working. Pediatricians like T. Barry Brazelton even extended the bonding period to one year, saying that the mother should definitely stay at home with her infant to insure school success, so the child would be able to get along with others, and to avoid delinquency (Eyer, 1992).

Bonding research placed women and children in the hands of the medical community, as dependent on hormones, chemistry, and crucial periods that would determine their fate. Eyer (1992) has described how the construction of bonding coincided with the need in "the psychological and medical professions ... to secure women and children as patients, and to find pathology in this clientele, which they could then treat" (p. 1). The concept was an extension of the attachment perspective that created mothering as predetermined and in need of scientific surveillance. Again women and children were made the objects of control and determinism. While veiled in the language of support for young children, the concept of bonding actually fosters a conservative universalist agenda that regulates women, predetermines human life, and pathologizes all those who do not fit within the construction (e.g., adoptive parents and children, males in general, and women who are not or do not choose to be nurturant).

Family Values
With continued emphasis on the mother, the family has been created as the site of early experience. Father and siblings have, to a minimal extent, joined the mother as responsible, especially for pathologies and abnormalities that science identifies as inflicting the child. As examples, the early experiences of a young child with a partially absent father are often seen as problematic; sibling rivalry is expected to cause problems for a young child in school; parents may be too firm or too lenient with their children, causing all kinds of problems. Additionally, the family is believed to be responsible for the young child's behavior (and by implication human behavior in society). Children are identified as coming from divorced, single-parent, motherless, and teen mother families. (Note the reference to mother in much of the terminology.)

Teen motherhood is an excellent example of this misplaced responsibility, especially in the United States where moral panic abounds regarding pregnancy outside of marriage. Yet, reasons for teen pregnancy appear similar to pregnancy for women over 20 (Phoenix, 1991); no relationships have been found between welfare and childbearing (Clark,

1989); most teen mothers and their children thrive well together (Furstenberg, Brooks–Gunn, & Morgan, 1987; King & Fullard, 1982). Both historically and presently around the world, first–time mothers are teenagers. However, teen pregnancy is blamed for multiple forms of childhood pathology. Offering appropriate early experiences is considered difficult if not impossible in these environments. We have constructed intervention systems ranging from parent education to removing the child from the home. Teen mothers are judged as those who may not provide the psychologically and medically determined appropriate experiences for their young children.

Psychology, social work, and medicine have joined to create teams of "experts" on how families should function with their children. In addition to mother/infant research, psychological investigations abound that focus on identifying the truth regarding appropriate early experience within the family. Families are expected to provide these prescribed quality experiences for their children, but the "what" and "how" of experiences are determined by experts from outside the family. These experts are most often middle class, educated, white, and male. Families whose experiences deviate from the expert perspective are considered deficient and in need of intervention.

Obviously tied to the enlightenment/modernist concern for the origins of human knowledge, researchers have constructed a line of study focusing on the "origins and growth of human competence." In 1974, Connolly and Bruner claimed that early experience determines competence in later life, indicting the family as the facilitator of this experience. Their conclusions were that middle-class child-rearing was necessary for adult success. Ghetto individuals were considered to be lacking in operative intelligence because of the lack of appropriate early experience. For example, ghetto black children were considered to have stunted mental growth because their parents transmitted an ideology of despair to them. In 1979, Burton White attempted to detail this focus on early experience, describing particular core behaviors that were necessary for what he called effective child-rearing. Altering the home for child exploration, spending time with the child on specific activities, providing play materials, availability to the child for several hours daily, and constructing a multitude of language experiences were included as core parental behaviors that resulted in advanced development. Connolly and Bruner proposed that there are either cultures of poverty or at least subcultures of despair in which families do not provide the appropriate "hidden curriculum" (p. 5). White, Kaban, and Attanucci (1979) proposed that if parents did not possess these essential skills, society should intervene to teach them.

John Ogbu (1981) has critiqued this perspective, pointing out that competency is constructed within a cultural context. Competent behaviors are not universal but originate based on adult tasks that are defined by a particular culture. Even middle–class white Americans have considered differing competencies to be important in different generations. At one point in time, self–control and self–denial were considered of utmost importance. Later generations have focused on getting along with others and self–confidence (Miller & Swanson, 1958). In dealing with children, the middle class often believe in reasoning and appeals to guilt while the working class often use physical punishment. This assertion of power may be necessary and beneficial if children are living in neighborhoods that are high in violence and danger (Brown, Martinez, & Radke-Yarrow, 1992). Ogbu reminds us that competencies and child–rearing may emerge within the life context as people use trial and error to learn to survive where they live. Researching families to determine universal early experiences that should be provided to all young children is at the very least ethnocentric. The concept of early experience is used to place dominant ideologies and the middle class in positions of power and legitimizes the identification as incompetent and the regulation of those families who do not conform.

Real Lives and Early Experience

Our son was adopted into our white, middle–class, educated family as a baby from India. What if he is identified or even diagnosed with "problems" during his life? Our current discourse on the role of early experience will either place his own biology or our family at "fault."

He just inherited the problems from his biological parents. Maybe they weren't very smart or had problems with language or reading.
He was institutionalized (in an orphanage and a hospital) for the first few months of his life.
He was not able to bond at the appropriate time with the appropriate parent.
His mother has always worked.
A white family should not adopt a child of color. They cannot provide appropriate experiences.

Our son's life would be predetermined in both the identification of problems and the reasons for those problems. Living within our current dominant perspectives, the creation of abnormality as a truth would not be questioned. The appropriateness of labeling him with a particular problem would be assumed. If the problem could not be denied, the societal conditions that constructed it would not even be considered. The discourse of appropriate early experience has constructed an environment in which some individuals are to be judged as not normal based on those experiences. Either the individual, the mother, or the family is blamed. The complexities of society and the power relationships that have both identified and subjugated that individual are denied.

Mother/Family Discourse and Determining the Life of the Child

Analysis of the historical construction of concepts of "mother" and "family" facilitate further understanding of why appropriate early experience emerged as a dominant discourse. We "talk" as if the nuclear, heterosexual family has always existed and that we have evidence as to its superiority, that the best place for children to thrive is in the arms of mother within this idealized family unit. Yet critical examination reveals that ideas of motherhood and family have varied in different historical periods, from generation to generation, in different cultural contexts, and have tended to be controlled by those in power. Experiences available to human beings of various ages have varied within these diverse contexts.

As evidenced by the attempts of political parties in the United States to be viewed as the party of the family (Egerton, 1991), political, popular, media, educational, psychological, and sociological discourses are all dominated by the language of the family. Within this language lie the assumptions that (1) the family is a universal entity that is necessary for all human beings, and (2) the foundation for the family is a heterosexual relationship (H. Marshall, 1991). Further, this normalized heterosexual relationship forms the nucleus to which biological children are added (Burman, 1994). Most recently the discourse has also included the claim to fundamental (American) values and socially accepted behaviors that would lead to happy, healthy, fulfilled family members, especially children. Family structures of various working– and middle–class minority groups, diverse household organizations (e.g., single–parent families, step–families, extended families), and nontraditional families (e.g., gay and lesbian families, racially mixed families, those who live together part–time) are either ignored or presented as abnormalities contributing to the problems of society (Collins, 1989; Patterson, 1992).

Since the 1960s, the family has been extensively researched from an empiricist, historical perspective that focuses on demographics (Vann, 1993). This research has tended to emerge from dominant discourses reproducing the established modernist order and/or reifying the family as universal. In 1979, Jacques Donzelot stated that a "critique of political reason" (p. 8) surrounding the notion of family was much overdue. Based on a Foucauldian ideology, he proposed that the history of the family be confronted as sociopolitical transformation, an uncertainty understood only within the multiple relationships that it maintains with society, and that society has forced upon it. Focusing mainly on French history, Donzelot's perspective led to an understanding of present–day family as the site of social regulation by the state, a form of policing. Further, in a complex manner, this family policing was accomplished by creating the child as the center. In the name of child freedom and protection, families were placed under surveillance and control by the state.

Policing Families

Before the eighteenth century, European families were both the subject and the object of government. The head of the family was accountable to the state for all of the family members (Donzelot, 1979; Mitterauer & Sieder, 1982). These family members (i.e., wife, children, relatives, servants and apprentices) were then answerable to the head of the family and were to function based on his decisions. Women, children, and servants were his property. He was responsible for paying taxes and providing labor and men for the military to the state in exchange for state protection and total discretion over his family. The smallest political organization of the family was therefore the state. Systems of honor, obligation, punishment, and favor were tied to member compliance with the head of the family. Families were the public world with no distinction between public and private (Donzelot, 1979).

Those not belonging with a family (e.g., vagabonds, beggars) were the challenge to the public order. Not only did no one supply their needs, but no one was in charge of controlling them. Led by this group and by family members who considered themselves to be victims of intense control, such complex events as the French Revolution developed. The family was positioned in the middle of beliefs that the state should meet the needs of citizens and the fear of a totalitarian regime. The role of the family within this changing context was questioned. In response, the family was transformed into a mechanism for regulation in the creation of a liberal definition of state.

The problem of the liberal state was seen as twofold: (1) the demand of the poor for work, education, and welfare, and (2) the diverse mores and living conditions exhibited by those who did not share bourgeois economic privileges and/or moral beliefs. How could these issues be addressed without the government taking charge? The solution was to transform the family in a way that would normalize the population through discourses of preservation and liberation specifically applied to children (Donzelot, 1979).

Alliance. Consistent with work in art and literature, by the middle of the eighteenth century, French physicians regularly wrote concerning the protection of childhood. The most common targets were foundling hospitals, domestic nurses raising children, and the servant–controlled education of rich children. The high death rate of foundling children was considered a loss to the state in that the individuals could be used in the military service, as soldiers in colonization. Children, whether foundling or children of privilege, were most commonly fed and raised by wet nurses. Physicians wrote that wet nurses were difficult to find, often took on too many infants at once, and even if working exclusively for a wealthy family were often self–interested and hateful. Servants of wealthy children were viewed as the natural enemy of the master (and his child who would become the master). Further, the servants were believed to be educating children for pleasure only and in ways of dress that were unhealthy and rendering them incapable of caring for themselves. Connected with the newly powerful medical domain, the protection and preservation of children became a discourse against house servants. Doctors constructed "household medicine" (Donzelot, 1979, p 16), in the form of techniques that would counter the negative effects of servants on children in bourgeois families. This household medicine appeared in books on child rearing, education, and medical care.

To control this medical advice and insure that it remained in the hands of physicians, family medicine was established. An alliance emerged between doctor and mother. Doctors viewed mothers as those who could be taught and would follow: "The role of the mother and that of the doctor are, and must remain, clearly distinct. The one prepares and facilitates the other ... The doctor prescribes, the mother executes." (Donzelot, 1979, p. 18)

Since this alliance appeared to favor the advancement of women by describing them as educable and useful, mothers welcomed it. Servants were closely supervised, bourgeois children were given a protected and closely observed freedom, and the bourgeois family constructed a wall against all outside influences. Further, this recognition of woman as mother, medical assistant, and educator supported feminist movements that emerged in the nineteenth century.

The children of servants and the poor were to be preserved through philanthropy which transmitted guidelines for behavior and established hygienic norms. Poor families were taught "scientifically" determined bourgeois self-sufficiency and were observed as to its accomplishment. Individuals were expected to adapt to hygienic behaviors viewed as preserving the liberal society — and, of course, its children.

Regulation. This appeal to the preservation of children and the resultant discourse can be easily compared to present–day beliefs in the necessity of appropriate early experience and the predominant responsibility of the family for this experience. The appeal results in the generation of both *disciplinary and regulatory powers* (Foucault, 1978). The discourses of disciplinary power are located in schools, hospitals, prisons, and the mass media, as well as fields like psychology and medicine. The behavior of individual bodies is controlled by creating the desire to be "normal." A standard is constructed by which individuals judge themselves. Although generally tied to health, this disciplinary power functions in the biologizing of childhood and the blaming of families. As examples, a women will naturally want to have and nurture children; if not, the women is not normal. Good mothers know how to play with their children; if a mother does not enjoy activities with young children, she is not a good mother. Childbirth is a medical condition requiring expert attention; those choosing to birth at home are not really concerned about the health of their children. Parents who are "sensitive" to their children will have happy, intelligent offspring; when parents are "insensitive," their children will exhibit pathology. This disciplinary power is concealed in a language that would have human beings become more useful, productive and powerful.

Actually, the individual or family may appear to gain power in that skills are developed that support the status quo and traditional society. (For a few, these skills could become sites of resistance.) However, these individuals also become more docile, judging themselves based on the truth constructed by the discourse, a subject of standards established by others, and limited to the expectations conceptualized within the power structure. For example, "my two-year-old is exploring 'his' 'identity' so I can't really keep him from coloring on the walls. Its only 'natural' for him to express himself."

Regulatory power is created through policies, laws, and interventions that would control and normalize. A state requirement for immunization before schooling is the most obvious form of regulatory power placed on families. Requiring teen mothers to live with their parents is another, perhaps more controversial, example. More subtle forms of control constructed around the education of children in the United States include readiness tests to determine the appropriateness of kindergarten entrance, school conduct policies that must be read and signed by parents, and state educational skills or essential elements that are imposed on all children. Whatever the family's preferred knowledge base, everyone is expected to conform to school regulations. The passage of a 1987 government act in England that referred to lesbian and gay families as "pretend families" (Burman, 1994, p. 68) constructs regulatory power demanding normality that has been determined by legislation and regulatory discourse. Regulatory power requires that all families yield to the forms of knowledge and ways of functioning in society that have been determined by particular power groups as appropriate.

Current family discourses are contradictory, positioning the family as both the savior of the child, and therefore the redeemer of society, and also the major threat to the continuation of a democratic society. Modern middle–class nuclear family values centering on the early experiences offered to children are presented as most appropriate and normal. Paralleling the French servant and the poverty–stricken populace, modern–day abnormal families (e.g., minority, poor, divorced, gay and lesbian, teen) are considered a threat to society, and therefore to their children. The transformation of the family and the construction of the child as the center of that family have emerged in a context in which the major concern is regulation. We have created parent and adult education, parent advice books, and regulatory measures grounded in the "progressive" perspective that we know more than previous generations (Jolly, 1981). Further, some of us know more than others about everyone's children and family. Developmental psychology and medicine have defined what is normal and what is deviant. Our concern has not been for younger members of society but how to regulate those who are different from us. How do we control those who do not believe what we do? How do we regulate those who act in the ways that our values specify as inappropriate? How do we keep them from hurting us economically? How do we keep them from contaminating our children? How do we teach them the right way? The family has become the site of this regulation whose goal is to make everyone believe, look, and function a particular way.

Constructing Motherhood

Critical analysis of French family history reveals how women, who had no power, were coopted by the medical profession in the move to expand and solidify its own power. In other time periods and in diverse cultures, views of women and their roles have varied. Grimshaw (1986) points out that the concept of women as nurturers of the emotions of others was not part of Greek philosophy. Further, Ruth Bleir (1984) has questioned the notion that women's work is universally accepted as biologically determined by the reproductive function. Women attempt to control reproduction rather than have their lives determined by it. For example, the !Kung women in the Kalahari Desert (and other women around the world) nurse their children for three years so they can maintain societal activities without pregnancy and childbirth (Burman, 1994).

True woman!? As with the family, ideas about motherhood have changed from generation to generation and certainly vary from culture to culture. What we in the United States and Europe think we know about mother–child relationships are actually constructions of a particular culture. The emergence of the "cult of true womanhood" (Eyer, 1992, p. 101) in the 1830s played a major role in the construction of our beliefs about motherhood.

Before the Industrial Revolution, women in the United States owned businesses, managed farms, and generally shared in the work of an agrarian society with men. Children were often wet–nursed and put to work for the household as soon as they could follow directions (Matthaei, 1982). As men moved into factory work, women also pushed to enter the world of industry. Because factories appeared brutal and men wanted a cushion from the marketplace, a rationale for keeping women at home emerged (Degler, 1980; Ehrenreich & English, 1978; Eyer, 1992; Lasch, 1977). As Barbara Welter (1979) explains, nineteenth century man soothed his conscience for seemingly abandoning the religious beliefs of his forbears by creating woman who would stay at home and hold to those values. Woman was constructed as hearth angel, "another better Eve, working in Cooperation with the Redeemer, bringing the world back from its revolt and sin" (pp. 177-178).

Women's magazines and religious literature proclaimed the "cult of true womanhood," describing feminine virtues as purity, piety, submissiveness, and domesticity. A division was created between the public and the private (Urwin, 1985), between male and female. Woman's identity was gendered as faithful and happy in the performance of family duties (Okin, 1989). Religious leaders referred to women as angel mothers and those who would keep the infant mind from evil. Women who pursued interests outside the home were labeled semiwomen and perverts (Welter, 1979).

As American motherhood was constructed by religion in the first part of the 1800s, the child was created by enlightenment/modernist discourses of reason and progress. (See Chapter 2 for a complete discussion.) By the close of the nineteenth century, biological, evolutionary, and social reform experts had emerged who believed in the universal, predetermined child and offered advice on raising that child. For example, in 1909 Ellen Key (a eugenist) published *The Century of the Child*, challenging women to focus on children for many generations in order to foster the progression of the truly complete superior man. As discussed previously, "the infant was seen as a kind of evolving protoplasm through which society adapted and progressed" (Eyer, 1992, p. 108). Mothers were presented as those who shaped that progress, who molded and formed the child.

Hated and medicalized. During this same time period, women were chastised by medical experts who believed that a woman's biological destiny is motherhood(Sawicki, 1991). Women using their energies for other activities were expected to produce offspring who were defective. To illustrate, at Harvard University, Dr. Edward Clarke concluded that the pursuit of higher education would result in the atrophy of a woman's uterus. Shocks to the nervous system, as imposed by large amounts of reading or study, would damage the body and inhibit reproduction (Ehrenreich & English, 1978; Rosenberg & Rosenberg, 1984). In the twentieth century, the religious construction of motherhood was overshadowed by this biological construction. The moral control of women that had begun with religion was now perpetuated through science.

By the 1940s and 1950s, the popularization of gender roles had become so widespread that men were regularly referred to as aggressive and logical while women were seen as emotional and passive (Dally, 1983; Eyer, 1992; Lasch, 1977). A growing misogyny tied to this polarization was further supported by views of motherhood as the root of pathology espoused by psychoanalysis and medicine. Mothers were believed to cause all problems. Mental illness in children was considered the result of mother's subconscious urges; this mental illness required correction by experts in psychology and the social sciences. Foundational work leading to the construction of "proper mothering" (covered earlier in this chapter) emerged in the writing of such researchers as Rene Spitz (1945) and David Levy (1944) blaming mother for everything from colic, to autism, to fecal play, to delinquency. Mothers were labelled overprotective, over-permissive, hostile, and moody. Philip Wylie (1942) even labeled mother (and by implication women) as power-hungry, cunning, and ruthless (Eyer, 1992). The importance of early experience as determining the life of the child emerged from a perspective in which women were hated and feared. The discourse provided a mechanism for blaming women and therefore, a reason for controlling them.

During World War II, women took over jobs (and dealt with multiple life situations) that had through the polarization of male/female roles been considered work that only men could handle. During this time, government advertisements that encouraged women to work also emphasized that this work was a duty to the men who were fighting, not an accepted new role for women (Eyer, 1992). Further, social scientists continued mother–blaming even referring to women as "war work deserters" because they were leaving their children behind (Barber, 1943, p. 170). As the war ended and men returned wanting jobs, women were told that only those who were wicked would work and attempt to manage the home. Mother blaming through concepts like maternal deprivation flourished and were illustrated in newspapers and popular child–raising books showing children placed in institutions and foster care. "Nothing since Victorian literature equaled the reverence with which women's magazines and related advice literature of the 1940s, 1950s, and 1960s extolled home and maternity" (Eyer, 1992, p. 124).

In a prominent book, *Modern Woman: The Lost Sex*, used in marriage and family college courses, Ferdinand Lundberg and Marynia Farnham (1947) described women as having given up femininity in a futile battle with men that resulted in delinquency or neurosis for their children. The feminist movement that had gained strength at the turn of the century and secured women's right to vote in 1920 was likened to communism and the Ku Klux Klan. Women were to return to submission and allow males to be the master (Eyer, 1992).

Freudians continued to hold mothers responsible for the adult personalities of their children and formally allied themselves with medical professionals to claim that women were naturally pathological, citing evidence ranging from premenstrual syndrome to pregnophobia to labor pains (Cooke, 1944; Eyer, 1992; Zilboorg, 1957). For example, postnatal depression emerged as a medical diagnosis. Feeling negative following childbirth was interpreted as an illness, an abnormality (Leach, 1988; Spock, 1988; Tizard, 1991). Interpreting such feelings as a medical problem denies women the right to feel negative about their children (which we all do about everyone at various points in our lives), masks the societal contexts that has placed impossible expectations on individuals, and denies the ways that we have isolated mothers and infants and provided them with almost no support (Nicholson, 1986).

Technological advances in medicine plus professional and corporate pressure to use these technologies, combined with parents who were choosing to have only one or two children, and resulted in the complete medicalization of pregnancy, childbirth, and early childhood growth and development. Parents were convinced that the one or two children would not be perfect, healthy, intelligent, and happy without medical intervention. Pediatrics emerged as a dominant force in discussions of early experience, especially as sophisticated technology constructed specializations like neonatology. Specialists like T. Berry Brazelton again dominated, describing the "maternal instinct" as naturally existing, necessary, and precious (Eyer, 1992).

During the twentieth century, mothers and children have been normalized by "expert" pediatricians and psychologists who have constructed a range of behaviors and development within which everyone is expected to fall. While we cannot deny the benefits of the medical profession, we must also admit that abnormality can be constructed as a mechanism for power, as a tool for disciplining and regulating others.

Minority women and children may prefer and need their own culturally constructed methods of childbirth and forms of child rearing; working class women may prefer and need older children to care for their younger siblings; middle class women and their children (perhaps the group that is most regulated by the fields of psychology and medicine because of peer and educational ties) may collapse with the guilt that results from living under such oppressive and impossible expectations (Rapp, 1987). The construction of early experience as the most important part of an individual's life denies the complexity of human beings, the problems with prescribing behavior for others, and limits possibilities for children.

Challenges to Dominant Ways of Thinking

I would not deny any life experiences as important to individual existence for all human beings. We cannot, however, ignore (1) the problems created by a discourse in which early childhood experience is considered the determiner of later life, or (2) the context, belief structures, and power relationships from which this discourse has emerged. To summarize this chapter, I would submit these complex issues as challenges to our construction of early experience and as reminders of the danger in unquestioned assumptions.

(1)   The belief that we know the early experiences that are most important for children oversimplifies their lives, constructs a context that privileges adults because we know what experiences they should have, and devalues the individual and group diversities with which human beings are blessed. We assume that the lives of younger human beings are so unsophisticated that we as more intelligent adults can uncover those lives.

(2)   When we assume that early experience determines the life of the child, we perpetuate the philosophy that there are discoverable truths which apply to all human beings and that one of those truths is linear human progress.

(3)   A belief in early experience as defining the life of the child is both deterministic and fatalistic. Not only do we believe that as

expert human beings we can determine what is appropriate for those who are younger than us, but we can identify those who are most likely to be lost because they did not have certain experiences.

(4)   The discourse of early experience emerged out of fear and the need to control the behavior of diverse and less powerful "others." At various points in history, both in Europe and in the United States, those with money have feared the masses. The poor have been created as those who are dangerous, whose behavior must be governed through standardization and regulation. Surveillance and intervention into private lives is legitimized because the "danger" must be controlled.

(5)   Various forms of misogyny underlie the construction of early experience. Women have been labeled as inferior, pathological, incapable of thinking for themselves, responsible for all of the problems in society, and definitely needing scientific regulation, all in the name of reproduction and child rearing. Science has generated woman's self–concept, morality, physical being, and appropriate behavior with their children and in relation to the rest of the world. The construction of early experience has been used to place impossible expectations on women and to blame them for not meeting those expectations.

(6)   Within the construction of early experience, children are created as an illness (see Bowlby's work) that must be regulated through scientifically defined activities. Further, the development of younger human beings was never the issue. Scientific investigations of knowledge, regulating poor and diverse populations, keeping mothers out of the work force, and controlling women were the issues.

(7)   In the name of early experience, children have been used by those who practice medicine, psychology, and social work to construct a context in which they are viewed as experts and therefore have power over others. They have created "abnormalities" that perpetuate their fields by providing a clientele of women,

children, and families. Further, the expertise that children and women possess concerning their own lives is denied.

(8)   The discourse of early experience has produced a normalized view of self and family that supports the status quo, marginalizing and pathologizing those whose views of early life experience (most often the poor and minority groups) are not the same as the accepted standard. Further, these normalized constructions become the standards from which individuals judge themselves and others. Questioning the standards is labeled pathological, deviant, or even radical.

(9)   Gender, class, racial, and age biases are clearly exhibited in the discourse of early experience, which has assumed male vs. female behaviors for adults, economic and time flexibility for families, universal human childhoods, and adult determination.

(10)   The belief that particular early experiences determine the life of the human being is ethnocentric, a belief not only in childhood but in one form of childhood.

(11).   Living within the discourse of early experience, complex societal problems are located within the individual (e.g., mother, child, poor) rather than examined as involving multiple power-relationships within a historical, social, political context. Society and State are thus eliminated from sharing in the responsibilities of life (e.g., neighborhood conditions, legal descrimination, the creation of privilege).

Not only have we constructed the concept of the universal "child" as a unique condition tied to development and progress, but the child has been created as a human being who needs particular life experiences. As Foucault (1983) has demonstrated, a discourse may either be liberating or oppressive, depending on the circumstance. A discourse may or may not be bad, but all discourses are dangerous, especially without examination. I would challenge all of us to continuously critique our construction of child and our focus on early experience. Does the construction create privilege and power for those of us who are older? Are younger human beings actually given greater voice within our construction, or do we speak for them? Does the construction generate greater freedom and increased social justice for diverse groups of people (e.g., young, old, women, children, poor, people of color), or does the construction result in increased power for those who already dominate (e.g., those with money and education, those who call themselves scientists)?

Finally, an examination of the concept of early experience would not be complete without focusing on the types of learning experiences that are claimed to be most appropriate, concepts like play and child–centeredness. This discussion has actually played a major role in the creation of the field of early childhood education and will be pursued in–depth in Chapters 5 and 6.

Chapter V

Institutionalized Stories of Education and Care

Curriculum is a disciplinary technology that directs how the individual is to act, feel, talk, and 'see' the world and 'self'. As such curriculum is a form of social regulation.

Popkewitz, 1996, p. 2

The image of "institutionalization" at first appears counter to the foundation of early childhood education. We are proud of our resistance to direct instruction, work sheets, and extended large–group methodologies. We focus on the needs of the child as the determiner of curriculum, insisting that child development be used as our foundation. We even construct parents as the child's first teachers. We consider early childhood education to be a field in which the child dominates. How could we be accused of sanctifying particular educational rules and perspectives about the world? After all, we place the child at the center of our attention and respond to that child as needed. There should be nothing institutionalized, or systematically established if the child is our focus of concern.

Yet, as we analyze the knowledge base in our field, our philosophy toward curriculum, how we think and talk about young learners, and the actual practice of early childhood education, we cannot ignore the singularity of perspectives that have constructed the field. Speaking in a single institutionalized voice, we advise parents, attend conferences, establish early childhood programs, and work with preservice teachers. Those who are accepted in the field, whether as teachers, teacher educators, or parents, speak a similar language and espouse similar educational practices. The voice is so strong that it silences those who would share diverse definitions of human relationships. Those who have been silenced include all children, as well as the poor, those with less schooling, and people from countries that have been labeled as "Third World." This dominant voice has silenced multiple views of education and learning. Further, in our institutionalized voice we have constructed a bureaucratic hierarchy through which we are all implicated as either functioning appropriately or inappropriately with younger human beings.

To understand the influences of early childhood education on diverse groups of people, both young and old, the stories of the field must be problematized. We must create ways in which those silenced voices can be heard. The purposes of this chapter are to identify the multiple sites of institutionalization within the context of early childhood education and to explore the power relationships generated from those sites. The knowledge base that has created the field, the language that dominates our professional interactions, and early childhood program implementation are used as locations for analysis.

Constructing a Knowledge Base: Psychological and Enlightened

Again rooted in enlightenment/modernist allegiances to science and reason, the field of psychology has dominated the knowledge base that has constructed early childhood education. The grand narratives of child development and modernist curriculum dominate the field. Although we have warmly accepted child development as grounding the field, early childhood educators often reject traditional educational curriculum perspectives that dominate elementary and secondary education as only narrowly tied to early childhood education. I would propose that we have basically, however, followed the same technical path constructed by educators working with older children. Some of our heros are different; some are the same, but their languages are similar. Overall, we have followed a technical path of curriculum development whether working with 4-year-olds or with early childhood preservice teachers. Child development and modernist curriculum perspectives are the knowledge bases that have constructed the field.

Child Development as Ethnocentrism

Clearly, institutionalized views of child growth and development have served as the dominant knowledge base for the field of early childhood education. One need only review educational philosophy statements, analyze child evaluation instruments or child development texts, or read position documents by early childhood organizations to see evidence of this focus on child development. We describe what children are like at particular ages (within a range) and what to expect as normal behaviors. Those of us in the field function in our literature and our behavior as if we know the truth about younger human beings, or that eventually our research will reveal that truth. The reader is referred to Chapter 3 for an in–depth discussion of the hidden assumptions underlying the construct. In this abbreviated section, child development is discussed as an institutionalized site of ethnocentrism and oppression.

Child development has ethnocentrically institutionalized a global child in the image of the Euro-American middle-class. To begin, the assumption that people are the center of the universe is a monocultural view (Popkewitz, 1996). Through child development, the child is constructed as progressing through stages of change that are revealed through scientific discovery and classified as social, emotional, cognitive, language, moral, and physical. The cultural belief in this universal human truth is not questioned. Additionally, human characteristics, competencies, knowledges, and possibilities that do not fall within this developmental construction are either ignored or disqualified as inferior or of little consequence. The child is also constructed as most easily progressing through these stages if allowed to explore the environment and mature naturally, with a minimal amount of adult interference. Material possessions and time for exploration are assumed. Those who do not find themselves in a materialistic environment in which leisure is possible are viewed as deficient. Faith in adult supremacy over child and reasoning over other forms of thought is dominant.

The construction of universal child development is a form of colonization, a cultural imperialism. Developmentalism places all children in positions in which others control them. Around the world, there are younger human beings who function as productive members in the survival of families. Yet, child development has constructed these people as incompetent, needy, and incapable. When diverse peoples within the same society contradict developmental expectations, they are labeled as needing expert guidance and intervention. When cross-cultural research reveals that all people do not follow normative child development expectations, those who are different are labeled as deficient. In contexts in which cognitive logic does not fit the expected norm, people are considered developing and not yet fully modernized. If physical skills appear above the expected norm, the physically advanced peoples are labeled as primitives who naturally acquire more advanced motor skills.

I am confident that early childhood educators honestly believe that a focus on child development has increased possibilities for young human beings and has made their lives more fulfilling and enjoyable. However, the time has come to recognize that this positivist, scientific construction has oppressed and will continue to damage children. Euro-American middle- and upper-class children are expected to live within the expectations that we have created for them even before they are born, limited to the possibilities that are within our institutionalized views of development. Children from cultures that are not Euro-American and those who are poor are automatically placed in the margin. Their unique knowledges, skills, abilities, and views of the world are denied.

Curriculum as Pedagogy as Subjugation

Although we have emphasized how early childhood education differs from the more rigid, didactic practices found in elementary and secondary education, a thorough analysis reveals that we are more alike than different. The various fields of education have shared a curriculum–development perspective, accepting the premise that particular content and experiences can be planned for learners that will lead to particular outcomes. Early childhood education cannot be completely divorced from other forms of United States and western education. In Weber's (1984) analysis, she locates early childhood education as rooted in the work of Plato, Comenius, and Rousseau, scholarship that is also tied to education for learners of all ages and to curriculum development focusing on planning, supervision, and evaluation. Froebel serves as an excellent example of a curriculum developer. Further, early childhood models of education not only put into practice the assumptions made by these philosophers, but follow the curriculum development tradition. The field of early childhood education, in conjunction with other fields, has institutionalized technical, deterministic perspectives of learning.

Sources of institutionalization. Because people are embedded in social, political, and historical contexts and continuously interact in complex human societies, no individuals are entirely responsible for ideas, languages, or sites of power that are generated. However, analysis of the ideas of particular individuals who have impacted the field is necessary, especially when focusing on the hidden assumptions and the beliefs that are not commonly politicized. Jean-Jacques Rousseau and Frederick Froebel are two such individuals who are by no means totally responsible for the field, but whose ideas require further examination and deconstruction. These individuals have at least dominated the discourse of both early childhood education and liberal constructions of curriculum. As Pinar, Reynolds, Slattery, and Taubman (1995) have suggested: "Before the Enlightenment, curriculum was assumed to be a spiritual journey; afterward, curriculum denoted a means of social engineering and progress" (p. 74). Although both Rousseau and Froebel were religious, neither advocated for formal religious doctrine. Their ideas strongly represent enlightenment allegiances to progress and social regulation.

Weber (1984) describes Rousseau as challenging the dominant focus on logic by proposing that reason is nothing without emotions. Further, Rousseau challenged the traditional Christian interpretation of the nature of man as evil by proposing that human beings are naturally good and "profoundly affected the thought of educational leaders that followed ... The key aspects of Rousseau's naturalism — freedom, growth, interest, and activity — radically departed from educational practice in the eighteenth century" (p. 28). In early childhood education, we have used Rousseau's work to place the child at the forefront of education. We espouse natural development, the goodness of children, and our need to protect them in the name of Rousseau.

But what of the assumptions underlying Rousseau's scholarly work? First of all, Kessen (1978) has thoroughly explained the complexity of Rousseau's ideas and the tendency of progressive educators to construct Rousseau as a patron saint while others label him as a villain. Both groups have misread and oversimplified the work. "To know what the received notions are upon any subject, is to know what those of Rousseau are not" (Kessen, 1978, p. 164). Because of the tiresome length of his writing, Rousseau 's work is often expressed in one-liners, "Man was born free...." or "God makes all things good...." (Kessen, 1978, p. 161), leading to a simplification of complex, contradictory, and even confusing ideas.

Since early childhood education has, however, institutionalized Rousseau as a champion of the child, the hidden messages within his ideologies require an at least minimal critical examination. Rousseau's messages were actually consistent with enlightenment discourses that generated dichotomous thought, faith in reason, and hierarchical human relationships. For example, constructing human nature as good perpetuates discourses that are dualistic. The natural goodness of man is simply the other side of natural evil. Emotion is constructed as truth that is the opposite of reason. As discussed previously, the child is the antithesis of the adult. Further, Rousseau clearly supported the belief in the supremacy of males and espoused conventional patriarchy (Taylor-Allen, 1982). Women were to play the role of nurturer, but fathers were the ultimate power. "In the same way that the real nurturer is the mother, so the real governor is the father" (Rousseau, 1983, p.71). Although Rousseau writes that his companion did not like the idea of giving up any of their five children to foundling homes, his wishes dominated. Each child was sent following its birth with not even a record of birth date or gender (Kessen, 1978).

Rousseau's belief in freedom was consistent with the covert construction of social regulation that has dominated the last three hundred years in western thought. Freedom is constructed as controlling others through language and veiled action. Although Rousseau proposed that children be given greater freedom — for example by eliminating the use of swaddles to bind the child — he also cautioned against spoiling. The child was to learn about his natural powerlessness, that he was a child and not an adult (Singer, 1992). "Let your pupil always believe that he is the master ... No other subjection is complete as that which keeps up the pretence of freedom; in such a way one can even imprison the will" (in Singer, 1992 quoting French version of Rousseau, 1983, pp. 130). Although credited with allowing the child to naturally grow and develop, the environments described by Rousseau were clearly prescribed and controlled by the adult. There existed an illusion of a natural environment. As examples, to teach him property rights, the teacher and the gardener destroyed Emile s work. Julie, the main character of his only work of fiction (McDowell, 1968), pretends to be called away in the middle of a story so that her child will teach himself how to read. Crocker (1968-73) labels Rousseau as a founding father of twentieth-century behaviorism, even to the use of "time out," contrived as a punishment by making all other places disagreeable. Rousseau believed in raising children to want only what was wanted by society, for strict obedience to laws that controlled societal corruption (Kessen, 1978).

What did Rousseau believe about younger human beings? This is a confusing and perhaps impossible question to answer. We can only question whether his focus led to any form of empowerment for children. First, he did send each of his five children to foundling homes as infants. When asked if that behavior proved that he hated children, he responded by blaming his partner as one who would have spoiled them and her mother as a person who behaved like a monster. The children most likely died because the odds of surviving for five years in a foundling home at that time were one in four. Rousseau labeled childhood the sleep of reason. As those who did not exhibit eighteenth-century adult reasoning, children were beneath man, primitives who were driven by impulse. Although he expressed his own discomfort in communicating with children, he believed that only with adult control could they be expected to adapt to society in ways that would eliminate social pestilence (Kessen, 1978). Aries (1962) points out that Rousseau foreshadowed contemporary constructions of childhood by associating younger human beings with primitivism, prelogicism, and irrationalism. Whatever Rousseau's beliefs, his discourses and ways of functioning clearly marginalize children as the "other," creating them as beings who are inferior, as those who must be controlled through laws that are covertly imposed through nature and reason. Rousseau's work has been institutionalized in our field as we have constructed our history, engaged in informal discourse, and formally accepted the work of such modern scholars as Piaget.

As early childhood educators, we trace our beliefs from Rousseau, through Pestalozzi, and to Froebel. A disciple of Rousseau, Pestalozzi placed a greater focus on the mother and portrayed the family as the site of social life, a belief that would be accepted by his student Froebel and applied to the construction of group education for young children. What of Froebel? Some say that although he originated the term "kindergarten" and created a curriculum, the field has gone beyond Froebelian beliefs. However, the evidence of institutionalization of his basic perspectives in both society and our field is strong enough to lead to an opposite conclusion.

Nineteenth–century feminists supported the work of Froebel in that women were not generally considered influential or competent in any sphere. "Feminine," emotional involvement was even considered a threat to the growth of enlightened reason in children. As with the medical profession (discussed in Chapter 4), the importance placed by Froebel on mothering generated a location of value for women that had not previously existed. The construction of the female as complimentary to the male, and therefore endowed with special female talents, opened public doors for some women. Creating a "spiritual motherhood," women who tied themselves to Frobelian perspectives wrote books, lectured, taught, and trained others in kindergarten pedagogy. They took opportunities that had not been previously available to them (Singer, 1992; Taylor-Allen, 1982).

On the other hand, Froebel's contribution (along with the work of female Froebelian pedagogues) became a site for the institutionalization of women as less than men, as those requiring training generated by the "expert" male even for working with children for whom they were ideally suited. Froebel first began his training for men, and only when they showed little interest did he admit women. Although Froebel believed that maternal love was the symbol of Divine unity, he stressed that women must be taught pedagogic skills, how to talk to children and ways to direct their play. He disagreed with the emancipation of women, wanting to have nothing to do with women who used education to obtain independence (Singer, 1992).

Froebel wrote that "women's love and children's love, children's life, child care and the female mind are one, according to their essence" (Froebel, in Singer, 1992, p. 53). The identities of women and children were so inextricably bound as to have no separateness. He even tied his ideas to faith in science by expressing the belief that child–rearing should be the science of women (Singer, 1992). His views reinforced the dominance of men over women and children, and the privileging of public over private that still exist today.

The popularization of the kindergarten movement in the United States foreshadowed the industrialization of early childhood education, the construction of three–dimensional definitions of learning by the capitalist world. "Educational" toys were created based on Frobelian "gifts" and became common household possessions in most middle–class homes.

The work of Rousseau, Froebel, and others (who were not necessarily discussed but whose assumptions could also be critiqued) was consistent with the social and political contexts of their times. However, in complex ways we have institutionalized this work as if it provided us with the truth that we should apply to everyone. Rousseau's work actually reinforces an acceptance of younger human beings as primitive, potentially subhuman because of their lack of western reason, and definitely beneath the adult male. Further, is a covert regulation of the human "will" by causing others to believe that they have freedom any less oppressive than direct control? Both men have perpetuated the western patriarchal dominance that has subjugated women and children for hundreds of years. Both constructed educational programs (one for single children with a tutor and the other for groups of children) that are consistent with notions of curriculum development that are technical and deterministic. This concept of curriculum development will be the next location in our search for sites of institutionalization in early childhood education.

Curriculum development: Pedagogy or subjugation. What is meant by curriculum development? Scholars locate the establishment of the field in a variety of contexts and circumstances. Hamilton (1990) focuses on enlightenment attempts to discover the origins of knowledge as well as the development of taxonomies and the fragmentation of knowledge into subjects. The term, from the Latin root, *currere*, has been defined as meaning everything from educational content and objectives to all of educational experience (Pinar, 1975). Some have even defined curriculum to mean pedagogy and many have defined it to mean learning content. Hamilton has located the use of the term in university records in the 1500s and 1600s as referring to "the entire multi-year course followed by each student" (1989, p. 45). The reader is asked to consider the possibility that both Rousseau and Froebel were early curriculum developers, contributing to the belief that a complex educational plan can transform "the crude raw material that children bring with them ... into a finished and useful product" (Kliebard, 1975, p. 81). Their ideas were constructed with the assumption that a particular set of values and ways of thinking could be transferred to the child and result in predetermined beliefs, values, and behaviors. This is both a common assumption and definitional to what is meant by curriculum development.

Pinar, Reynolds, Slattery, and Taubman (1995) have placed the beginning of the contemporary American curriculum field in 1928 with the publication of the Yale Report. An attempt to analyze undergraduate education in American colleges, this report described the aims of education to be the expansion of the mind and the acquisition of increasingly more information. Influenced by the belief that mental discipline is developed through the study of the classics, nineteenth century instruction emphasized reading and memorization. As the field of curriculum development emerged, these assumptions remained strong, but additional ideas, relationships, and events also affected its construction. An attempt to describe the entirety of historical, political, and social influences on the field of curriculum development would be beyond the scope and purpose of this book. (The interested reader is referred to *Understanding Curriculum* by Pinar et al.) This discussion is restricted to those curriculum perspectives that have been institutionalized as truth through the field of early childhood education, as well as in other areas of education.

The first idea is choice of knowledge or "what knowledge is of most worth?" (Spencer, 1860). Spencer proposed that curriculum does not involve the use of all knowledge, but represents a selection. Through appropriately selected curriculum, social progress can be promoted. Not only has this perspective been institutionalized through early childhood education, but it has grounded the philosophy of the field. As programs have emerged, early childhood education has accepted the knowledge de jour, whether hygiene or morals in the nineteenth century, psychodynamic interpretations of the social and emotional in the first half of the twentieth century, or cognition in the later half. Further, curriculum purposes have generally been to advance the individual and/or society. The most recent focus on developmentally appropriate practice reveals how thoroughly the notion has been institutionalized.

How could the selection of knowledge and a focus on social progress generate power for some and be oppressive to others? The obvious issue is knowledge; perhaps less obvious is social progress. The assumption that particular knowledge is worth more than other knowledge privileges those who possess that chosen information, those exclusive skills. The notion creates a power hierarchy in which that all–important knowledge is chosen (or discovered) by a particular group and others are expected to yield to the power groups decision. Additionally, the universal, predetermined truth of knowledge is assumed. No consideration is given to the possibility that knowledge may be socially constructed and different in different times, contexts, and situations. Education as predetermined knowledge is assumed. The possibilities for indeterminacy, multiple voices, multiple knowledges, and multidirectionality are not considered. Further, attempts to determine the "best" curriculum knowledge reinforces the notion of progress (Munro, 1996). Social progress is a complicated issue that is discussed throughout this book. The curricular assumption that human beings need to progress gives power to those who are deciding the definition of progress and labels as inferior those who do not meet those progressive assumptions. Popkewitz (1996) illustrates in defining curriculum as "an invention of modernity that ... involves forms of knowledge whose functions are to regulate and discipline the individual " (p. 10).

The second curriculum perspective that is institutionalized within early childhood education is child–centeredness. Child study and developmental psychology served as the foundation for those who focused on younger human beings rather than subject knowledge. Borrowing ideas from

Pestalozzi and Froebel, Colonel Francis Wayland Parker proposed that the child is the center of the curriculum and that schools represent embryonic democracies (Parker, 1894). Called the father of the progressive movement by John Dewey (Pinar et al., 1995), Parker practiced an integrated form of natural teaching that placed the child at the center. Although Parker generated the most attention as an educator, those who pursued the scientific study of the child have also advocated for child–centeredness, placing knowledge of the child's growth and development at the center of the curriculum. The institutionalization of child–centeredness through early childhood education is obvious in our language to each other and parents, in philosophical statements, in our focus on play, and in the methodologies that have been labeled child–centered.

Most of us have felt that if we want children to be equitably treated and valued as human beings, child–centeredness makes the most educational since. We might ask, how child–centeredness could be oppressive. However, from the discussion of Rousseau's perspectives, one could argue that child–centeredness is not always what it would appear to be on the surface. Further, the underlying assumptions that construct the concept are only beginning to be examined. An–indepth discussion of these assumptions can be found in Chapter 6. Points that can be listed here include (1) the covertly deterministic nature of child–centeredness and (2) the construction of educational truth. Child-centeredness does not turn education over to younger human beings but constructs both the child and an environment in which predetermined educational objectives are less obvious. Child-centeredness inscribes rules about the child's construction of "self"; the child does not make this determination (Luke, 1989). Further, those whose past experiences do not represent middle–class forms of exploration are placed in a position in which they must guess what is expected of them (Delpit, 1995). Middle–class, white children most often come to school with experiences that are consistent with the notion of child–centeredness and are therefore placed in a position of identification and privilege. The construction of child–centeredness as the way in which children learn creates the same truth that is implied by direct instruction as the one method of learning; there is one truth about how children learn. The creation of one truth is positivist and does not allow for multiple perspectives or multiple truths.

The final perspective that has been institutionalized through early childhood education is the organization of educational experience as proposed by Ralph Tyler. Education in general, as well as early childhood education, has embraced the assumption that learning only occurs for groups of people when goals, objectives, learning experiences and evaluation are organized and preplanned. In fact, Davis (1986) has explained that the curriculum field actually emerged as curriculum development, but was shortened in terminology (not philosophy) to curriculum. Development obviously implies linearity and progress. The truth of the organization and the necessity of each component are not questioned.

Constructed as a syllabus for a course at the University of Chicago, Tyler's book *Basic Principles of Curriculum & Instruction* (1949) is probably the most influential text written in curriculum (Pinar et al., 1995). Tyler focused on four issues: (1) selecting and defining learning objectives, (2) selecting learning experiences, (3) organizing learning experiences, and (4) evaluating learning. We see continued evidence of Tyler's principles throughout early childhood education even today in the construction of curriculum guides, course syllabi, evaluation instruments, and even in discussions of developmentally appropriate practice. Scope and sequence are assumed necessities. In most of our teacher education programs, we have constructed success as dependent on the preservice teachers ability to preplan, usually in writing. Lesson plans and units dominate educational programs. Although Tyler's approach has been critiqued and criticized over the last twenty years, we have institutionalized the belief, in one form or the other, that educational goals must be predetermined, learning experiences preplanned, and evaluation conducted.

How are power relationships generated through the organization of educational experience? First, the rational development of curriculum is rooted in the scientific, linear, deterministic enlightenment beliefs discussed throughout this book. The beliefs are used to construct the "learner" as a universal being, a human truth regardless of time, space or geographic location. The application of educational goals/objectives to learners constructs changing behavior as the purpose of education. Within this educational purpose, societal political and power structures are denied and the rational individual is constructed as the source of change (Thomas, Myer, Ramirez, & Boli, 1987). The creation of goals and objectives is a norm–based activity (Kliebard, 1987). The group of people who decide on educational goals are immediately given power over those who must attain the objectives and those who do not meet the norm. A disciplinary power is generated in which meeting the norm becomes the foundation for human worth.

In planning learning experiences, the assumption is made that the teacher can control the learning environment (and by implication even the interactional behavior of the learner) in such a way as to achieve particular outcomes. This Pavlovian perspective ideologically gives total control to the teacher (Kliebard, 1975), whether through direct instruction or hidden within the discourse of child–centeredness. Planning learning experiences, especially with the assumptions that the outline will actually be followed, is obviously deterministic and gives no voice to the human beings who are to be "educated."

Finally, evaluation has been constructed as a form of product control, closely tied to industrialization and the creation of an end product. Evaluation, as a construct, assumes that learning has a predetermined, terminal point. Educators espouse life–long learning, but when using evaluation actually function as if learning ends. Further, the concept is normative, whether the standard is group behavior, individual child development, or comparison of how the individual has behaved in the past; acceptable norms are assumed. Defined as the goals, organization, and evaluation of educational experience, curriculum development perpetuates the social regulation and limitation of human beings through education.

Curriculum models. Various curriculum development activities have yielded early childhood models of education. In addition to the Froebelian curriculum, Montessori's work in Italy and the British Infant School are most often included along with Head Start and Follow Through models of education. The models are presented as philosophically distinct, representing behavioral, social, cognitive or other orientations. Yet, all have been conceived within a sociopolitical context in which a psychological view of children is used to create learning experiences that are purported to result in particular outcomes, a linear, Tylerian educational philosophy. For example, a Piagetian constructivist goal is to promote "children's decentration from a single perspective to consider and try to coordinate multiple perspectives"(DeVries & Zan, 1994, p. 105). Learning experiences are suggested and evaluation is assumed in the construction of the goal.

Essentially, all models use the same knowledge bases, institutionalized curriculum development and psychological theory. Within the construction of "model" is the acceptance of curriculum development represented by goals, prescribed learning experiences, and evaluation. Whatever the philosophy, the construction of a model assumes that educational outcomes can be predetermined. Constructing a model demonstrates the acceptance of the reductionist notion (a knowledge base) that we can a priori construct educational experiences that will lead to particular educational outcomes (Silin, 1987). The Piagetian describes children as internally constructing their own understanding through equilibration processes and the establishment of reciprocal relationships. The behaviorist describes children as changing through behavior modification, reward, and outside control. The followers of Montessori describe the child as one who uses exploration to fully develop brain function and continually adapts to the environment (Lillard, 1996), and on and on. Essentially, all models use the same knowledge base. All models assume that the child exists as a psychological being whose human characteristics can be scientifically determined, and that educational truth is a reality.

Institutionalized Language: Creating Others With Our Speech

Foucault, Derrida, and others have written about power and language, about the ways in which language constructs our lives and what we believe. In addition to discourses that promote particular ideologies, even the ways in which various languages like English, Chinese, or Russian are constructed reflect particular views of the world. Forms of discourse are not our own, but have emerged from complex historical, social, and power contexts. As Popkewitz (1996) explains, "when we 'use' language, it may not be us speaking. Our speech is language historically formed and when brought into the present ... overpopulated with the intentions of others" (p. 17). In a sense, this entire book is about the institutionalized language or discourse of early childhood education, yet it is impossible to fully examine language as a site of institutionalization because even the language that we learn as infants has been constructed through a particular ideological and cultural lens. The language that we use to "examine language" is a cultural construction.

The purpose of this section is to introduce institutionalized language constructs that we may not have directly recognized as part of our constructed world, briefly describing the hidden assumption(s) within each concept, and the potential influence of the use of the concept on various

human beings. In early childhood education we have functioned as if
constructs like child, development, and early experience are human truths.
In Chapters 2 through 4, these discourses have been analyzed as social
constructions that do not necessarily represent truth for all human beings.
In this chapter, the language of curriculum development that fosters the
belief in goals, plans, and evaluation is critiqued. In Chapter 6, the
discourses of child–centeredness and play are examined. The following are
additional examples of institutionalized language constructs that we have
accepted in early childhood education as truth without question or analysis.
The list is minimal, offered to provide the reader with possibilities for
critique. I would hope that with our focus on deconstruction and
problematization in this volume, the reader would choose many other
language constructs that require investigation.

Active Learning/Concrete Materials

The concept of active learning is created from a dichotomous
perspective that constructs humanity oppositionally: good/evil,
reason/emotion, male/female, adult/child, white/black, straight/gay,
concrete/abstract, active/passive. Active is good; passive is bad. Further,
the concept implies that we can name the truth about learning, and identify
and categorize that truth for human beings. The notion of active learning
implies that some group of experts can determine for "others" what is
active and what is not, and that for the well-being of those others experts
must make the determination for them. Further, the notion suggests that the
human body is compartmentalized with a brain that categorizes experiences
as active or passive and that we know the "truth" regarding that brain, an
expression of the ultimate belief in a truth revealed by science. These same
assumptions are prevalent in the focus on concrete materials as the medium
for learning, best for those who are younger and for those who are
approaching new concepts. The universal reality of concreteness versus
abstraction is assumed and the expert is given power in the construction of
that differentiation. How can I assume that the world is separated into
active or passive experiences, concrete or abstract materials, much less that
I could determine these categories for other human beings?

Classroom Management

Perhaps more than any other term, the notion of management illustrates
the historical purpose of schooling and adult constructions of younger

human beings. Schooling was constructed to control particular groups; management is the language of that control. As long as management is a major theme in education, we as educators will have difficulty with management and control. We will continue to think about how to control others. A current example is the debate in teacher education over whether management courses should be part of course work in preservice education. Generally, one side has insisted on the creation of a management course in which everything from discipline to organization of materials to communication characteristics of particular groups is included. The opposing side has proposed that management should be integrated throughout all course work and that good teaching will solve many management problems. Neither side has recognized that they speak the same language. No one problematizes the construction of schooling as a control mechanism. Perhaps as long as schooling is conceptualized as control and the discourse of classroom management is used, management will be an issue. Placing other human beings in an institutionalized setting in which they are to be controlled will probably always result in management problems.

Learning Style

The creation of a learning style construct assumes scientific discovery of learning as a human truth that can be identified and categorized. Universal human learning, whether one type, five types or ten types, is assumed. Further, particular groups of human beings (e.g., educational psychologists, learning style researchers) are placed in the position of judging the universal human characteristics of others. Social construction, cultural values, and historical/political context are all denied. Constructed from within the dominant perspective that purports scientific identification of human truths, the notion of learning styles actually reinforces the status quo. For example, defining a particular group such as African Americans as generally exhibiting a social learning style constructs stereotypes and reinforces the dominant belief in predetermined human truth. Of even greater concern, the categorization positions children of color as the "Other," those who are not normal.

Outcome(s)

In the past, multiple terms have been used to give the same meaning as outcome(s). We have used the words objectives, aims, goals; less directly, discourses of skills and competencies have been created. They all imply the same enlightenment/modernist belief that we can predetermine the lives of others by constructing experiences in a linear fashion based on a scientific truth about human beings, that we can control the future and regulate other human beings. All represent a positivist language that implies predetermination, one truth, and control by a particular group. Even when admitting to the uncertainty of the future, and when espousing child construction of meaning, we as educators have continued to speak the language of outcomes, of predetermined end points in our educational activity. This language does not allow for ambiguity, uncertainty, freedom, or the construction of multiple new worlds and ways of being. The language perpetuates determinism, control, and the status quo.

Parent Involvement

Parents are already involved in the lives of their children, in multiple ways and in multiple forms. By constructing the language of "parent involvement," educators place themselves above both younger human beings and their parents as those who possess the accepted knowledge that must be revealed to "others." We must show parents how to be involved with their children, with the school, with appropriate early experience, with homework, — in short, how to manage their children. Educators (and I include myself) have not constructed a language that gives the message that we want to learn from and with parents and their children. The hidden, yet dominant assumption in the words "parent involvement" are that parents are not involved and do not know how to be part of the lives of their children. The discourse immediately places parents in the margin and constructs power over them by those who are in the field of education.

Self-Concept

The focus on self–concept is a veiled method of privileging the western (and predominantly American) notion of individualism, yet denying societal responsibility for social justice and the human condition. The "self" represents that decontextualized body that is responsible for growth, progress, reason, truth, and values. The individual self must be strong and disciplined, and must believe in its own worth because, with a focus on individualism, there are not other resources. The notion of self–concept is patriarchal, privileging western forms of male detachment. The assumption that all humans can and should work toward an individually oriented positive regard, an autonomous being, privileges those cultures that focus on individualism and disqualifies those cultures, groups, families, and even individuals who do not construct humanity as a group of separated beings.

Institutionalizing Inequality: Early Education
as a Two-Tiered World

The construction and application of education in the form of schooling has virtually always been a two–tiered system whose purposes led to privilege for some and control of others. Plato's conception of education was for those who would be leaders, not for everyone. In eighteenth– and much of nineteenth–century Europe and the United States, even as white European and American males were exposed to a variety of forms of schooling, females were either given no opportunities or cautioned to limit intellectual pursuits lest their reproductive capacity be curtailed (See Chapter 4.). Under slavery in the United States, Blacks were forbidden from attending school or attaining any of the skills that were offered through formal schooling upon penalty of death. When education was offered to the poor, it was grounded in the assumptions that individuals and families were deficient and that the state must "expertly" regulate and control the behavior of those in poverty. Education, in one way or the other, has been one site for the generation and perpetuation of race, class, and gender inequity and the construction of power hierarchies.

This tiered system is directly illustrated in the practice of early childhood education over the past two hundred years. First, the field emerged from within a historical context in which the regulation of poverty and the control of immigrants has been and is of utmost importance. Clear examples of this can be found both in the past and present. In discussion of schools for the working class, Adler illustrates: "Let us use what influence we have to correct the false idea of equality ... Let us impress upon the minds of the children that the business of life will always be carried on in a hierarchy" (Barnard, 1890, p. 681). In the marketing of their own preschool model, Schweinhart and Weikart state "The results are in. High-quality, active learning preschool programs can help young children in poverty ... to become economically self-sufficient, socially responsible adults" (1996, p. 338).

Education as the Perpetuation of Racial/Class Bias

Those of us who would be called early childhood educators consider programs for children under 8-years-old to be within the purview of the field. Nursery, kindergarten, and child care programs were not, however, constructed as equivalent forms of early education or for purposes of serving all children. The majority of programs that have constructed the field have focused on guiding particular groups of human beings toward normalcy, toward overcoming the diversity that is not consistent with dominant views of human life, family, and ways of functioning. Early childhood programs have institutionalized the belief that particular groups of people are inferior to others.

Sites of institutionalization. In the United States, early childhood programs have for almost two hundred years been predominantly supported by a fear of poor, immigrant, and culturally diverse populations. Consistent with the rise of philanthropy as a mechanism for the guidance and control of poor populations described by Donzelot in Europe (see Chapter 4), charity schools emerged in the United States in the early 1800s to rectify deficiencies that were believed to exist within the home and to guide children in American citizenship. Sunday Schools were begun by the wealthy who believed that the poor spent their Sundays wastefully and needed guidance in virtuous behavior. Urban private and public primary schools, similar to religious schools for the poor in Europe, included 3-, 4- 5-, and 6-year–olds who were monitored by older children. Infant schools, extensively supported by ladies' charity organizations, were open to children as young as 18 months. Although promoting more nurturant, informal environments than primary schooling, the purpose of the infant school remained the philanthropic guidance of poor and immigrant children. Children from wealthier backgrounds were not included in the construction of these programs for young children because those in power assumed that a natural home environment with quality mothering, as provided by wealthier families, was the best situation for a child (Bloch, 1987).

Although the nurturant methods used in the infant school began to attract wealthier families, the interest faded. Critics during the 1840s proposed that education outside the home would damage young children, leading to epilepsy and even insanity. Since the infant school had been treated as a fad by philanthropists, support was soon withdrawn.

As the infant school declined, Froebel's work gained attention in both Europe and the United States. Between 1870 and 1880, over four hundred kindergartens and ten kindergarten training schools were established in the United States. Emerging as a popular form of mission work for young wealthy women, kindergarten was viewed as the best way to save children (Vandewalker, 1908). This Froebelian kindergarten was popular in the United States for over fifty years especially as a maternal play substitute for poor children (Bloch, 1987).

By the end of the nineteenth century, day nurseries had been established by philanthropists and middle–class social reformers as child care for poor mothers needing to work (Steinfels, 1973). Because the belief in the home as the best environment for young children continued to dominate, even founders of the nurseries viewed families who needed child care services as pathological. Poor, immigrant, and culturally different families were considered deficient, unable to maintain a conventional home life and in need of instruction in hygiene and basic functional skills. Day nursery workers therefore stressed hygiene, moral values, and strict schedules and denied the child care service to those who did not obey (Wrigley, 1991).

During the beginning of the twentieth century, early childhood teachers and psychological "experts" began to discuss group programs for privileged children. Recognizing that families of privilege seldom needed child care and that the middle–class home was considered ideal for children, these advocates emphasized the scientific knowledge that could be provided through a nursery school environment. Nursery schools for children of privilege were promoted as programs in which teachers were experts in the newly "discovered" science of child development. These teachers were presented as experts who could establish an environment that would maximize a child's developmental potential and even share this information with mothers (Howes, 1923; Kitchen, 1935). The programs were private and often attached to research facilities and universities. The middle–class accepted this scientific "professional" knowledge as a way of providing enrichment for their children.

Because of both the Depression and World War II, the federal government in the United States played a major role in child care during the 1930s and 1940s. To some extent, government construction of programs reduced the stigma of assistance that had been associated with day nurseries. However, as a general practice, more privileged children continued to attend private nursery schools. Poor children attended the government funded programs that basically ended by the 1950s as mothers were pressured to leave the work force to return home as the "good mother" (Wrigley, 1991).

The establishment of Head Start in the 1960s reinforced the already institutionalized two–tiered system. As Robert E. Cooke, chair of the planning committee, stated years later, the purpose of Head Start was "to interrupt the cycle of poverty, the nearly inevitable sequence of poor parenting which leads to children with social and intellectual deficits" (Cooke, quoted in Wrigley, 1991, p. 196). Created to provide early experiences for children living in poverty, the program was grounded in the assumption that particular groups of children are deficient, that parents are responsible for these deficiencies, and that outside intervention is necessary to overcome the problems.

As with the enlightenment/modernist focus on human reason and unquestioned faith in science, the development of the child's intellect was the major goal. Head Start would provide an environment in which "disadvantaged" children would become like their middle–class peers, would be prepared cognitively for first grade. Day nursery philanthropists constructed groups of people whom they considered deficient in hygiene, the new science of the day. Child advocates of the later twentieth century constructed groups of people that they considered deficient in cognitive and intellectual growth. The poor, and often those who are culturally or racially different, have been constructed as deficient in whatever human characteristic dominated scientific study of the period (Wrigley, 1991).

The belief in "good mothering" was extended in the establishment of Head Start programmatic requirements for the development of close ties to families. At the beginning, some groups of parents influenced and even controlled the programs. However, as administrators and politicians realized that parents were constructing curriculum, they created restrictions. Parental control was reduced. Not unlike the parent education focus of the day nurseries, Head Start was designed with the assumption that parent behaviors must be changed. Parents were to learn about hygiene, nutrition, and how to communicate with and provide learning experiences for their children.

What of children who were not from the disadvantaged class? Preschools and nurseries for the middle class have continued to function and grow. However, the programs have been constructed around notions of enrichment and the development of full potential. Although psychological science has generated cognitive goals for all children in early childhood programs, middle–class children have not been judged based on cognitive measures. They have not been constructed as human beings who are deficient and needing intervention, but as curious, intelligent, and responsive to enrichment.

Issues of power. Since the programs that have contributed to the construction of this two–tiered system are either philanthropic or government funded, critique creates a situation in which we run the risk of being used by economic conservatives as an excuse for eliminating programs. The critical issues are not the creation and funding of special programs. The issues are the ideologies that are promoted by the ways that those programs are conceptualized and the long–term power effects on the lives of human beings "served" by the programs. Clearly, from one perspective, we can point to how particular programs have directly saved the lives of some younger human beings. From a more critical vantage point, we must stress that the creation of a program for one particular group (1) lays the blame for societal problems on that group, rather than the larger power structures within the society as a whole, and (2) legitimizes the belief that one group of human beings is inferior to another. We have not stood for programs that are all inclusive and without stigma.

For two hundred years, poor, immigrant, and culturally different groups of children and their families have been considered deficient and needing intervention and instruction in how to live their everyday lives. The middle–class way of life has been constructed as the standard for everyone. This perspective has disqualified the knowledge(s) of those who do not espouse middle–class values and beliefs and constructed a message that these "Other" people and their children are inferior.

Early childhood programs have perpetuated this institutionalized belief in others as inferior by functioning as a socioeconomically segregated system. The poor are placed in subsidized programs while the affluent are served by private programs. The groups do not commonly interact with each other. Further, the curriculum is viewed as designed to eliminate deficiency in one and to develop full potential in the other. We have clearly institutionalized different early childhood educations for different groups of children and their families.

Institutionalized Early Education and Care:
The Construction of Power

Early childhood education as a field has sanctified particular knowledges, rules, and constructions of the world that have negatively influenced particular groups of human beings. Programs, curricular perspectives, and discourses, although often constructed with the best of intentions, have generated sites of power through which particular groups are institutionally perceived as second–class citizens, deficient, uneducated, or generally lacking. The following are reminders of some of those sites of power.

(1)   The acceptance of child development as universal truth has institutionalized notions of the "global" child in the image of the Euro-American middle class, marginalizing both the poor and cultures that do not appear western. Further, all younger human beings are limited by our institutionalized views of how they are to "be" in the world.

(2)   The "champions" of the child (e.g., Rousseau, Froebel) have constructed views of younger human beings in which patriarchal dominance is accepted. As examples, foundational to Rousseau's work is the covert regulation of the human "will" by creating the illusion of choice. One group is constructed to willingly yield to another. Although women were inseparably tied to children, Froebel believed that women must be taught how to work with children by those who are more advanced in such matters. Again, one group is legitimized as superior to another.

(3)   Early childhood education has institutionalized the assumption that particular knowledges are more valuable than others and that those valuable knowledges lead to social progress, for example, Piagetian constructivism. A power hierarchy is constructed by those who hold the "valuable" knowledge over those who do not or over those who disagree.

(4)   The institutionalization within early childhood education of the notion of child–centeredness actually perpetuates a form of covert

control and creates the same positivist truth that is implied by direct instruction: that there is one method through which everyone learns.

(5)   Early childhood education has functioned with the Tylerian belief that goals must be predetermined, learning experiences preplanned, and evaluation conducted. For evidence, one need only observe teacher education courses, curriculum guides, professional documents, teacher–created learning centers, and actual classroom practice. Through traditional curriculum development perspectives, education has been institutionalized as a norming activity that gives power to those who construct the norm and places the blame on the individual child or teacher. A disciplinary power is generated in which meeting the norm becomes the foundation for human worth.

(6)   Although presented as philosophically distinct, early childhood models of education use the same knowledge bases; institutionalized forms of curriculum development and psychological theory. Further, whatever the philosophy, the construction of a model assumes that educational outcomes can be predetermined and that the child exists as a psychological being whose characteristics can be revealed through science.

(7)   In early childhood education (and education in general), we use multiple forms of discourse that construct educational truths that are accepted as universal without question or recognition of the political and power context from which they have emerged. The constructs and ideas that are part of our language serve to privilege particular groups, normalize and marginalize others, and perpetuate the status quo.

(8)   Early childhood education has virtually always been a two–tiered system in which one from of education is provided to the poor, to children of color, and to immigrants while another form of education is provided to children of privilege. Further, the curriculum has been and is viewed as designed to eliminate deficiency in one group and to develop potential in the other.

Whether we like the ideas or not, early childhood education has played a role in the continued segregation of different groups of people, in societal beliefs in particular groups as inferior, and in the perpetuation of power for those that would control the lives of others. In the following chapters, the field is further critiqued as child–centered, play–based instruction and professionalism are analyzed.

Chapter VI

Privileging Child-Centered, Play-Based Instruction

with
Radhika Viruru

Child–centered pedagogy is just as coercive as traditional approaches but in more subtle ways ... underlying the model of the romantic, natural, innocent child lies an image of children as destructive, asocial and therefore threatening to the social order.

Burman, 1994, p. 170

Rooted in the work of Rousseau, Pestalozzi, and Froebel, contemporary early childhood educators have constructed child–centered instruction as the form of learning that is both natural and appropriate for all younger human beings. We focus on the "whole child" and communicate with language that would address child interests, needs, and development. We envision classrooms in which children create their own stories, choose activities from a variety of materials and learning centers, regulate their own behavior, progress from less to more advanced thinking, and, of course, are happy and healthy. We tell parents that play is the young child's work and encourage parents to play with their children. Teachers are viewed as guides and advisors in a flexible and fluid learning environment that responds to the natural development of children (McNally, 1974) and is perceived as promoting a democratic society (Walkerdine, 1988). We have tied this belief in child–centeredness to definitions of quality teaching through the promotion of developmentally appropriate practice, in accreditation, and in the construction of early childhood teacher education programs. Early childhood educators would most likely ask how anyone could fault the notion of child–centeredness.

Hopefully obvious to those who have read the first five chapters in this book, child–centered pedagogy perpetuates the dominant ideology that reifies a universal child and describes that child as progressing through predetermined stages of human development. Child–centeredness becomes the universal human pedagogy that is appropriate for all human beings, the truth for everyone. We have already considered the power issues and the disqualification of diverse knowledges that underlie the construction of one human truth. Less obvious is the notion that child–centered pedagogy is a structured form of human regulation. Further, the tenets of child–centered pedagogy are dominated by veiled assumptions regarding democracy, human nature, and the circumstances of human life. In this chapter, child-centeredness will be examined and problematized as a modern pedagogical practice that reproduces the cultural capital of the dominant group, fosters specific forms of adult and socioeconomic privilege, and oppresses particular groups of children and adults.

The Construction of Child–Centered Pedagogy

Child–centeredness is conceptually located in the work of eighteenth– and nineteenth–century philosophers as well as the educational practices proposed by Maria Montessori, Susan Isaacs, Margaret Lowenfeld, and John Dewey (Burman, 1994; Singer, 1992). As discussed in Chapter 5, Colonel Francis Parker argued most loudly the case for child–centeredness during the later part of the eighteenth century. Borrowing from Froebel's belief that play is the method used by young children for learning, Parker published *Talks on Teaching* (1883) and *Talks on Pedagogics* (1894). In his work as an educationist in Quincy, Massachusetts, and in Chicago, Illinois, Parker placed this natural, play–oriented child at the center of the curriculum. Consistent with the acceptance of natural scientific truth, the child was constructed as the heart of the educational process through the belief that natural forms of education were best and that the school represents an "embryonic democracy" (Parker, 1894, p. 423).

Rejecting both rote teaching methods and behaviorist models, child–centeredness provided educators with a pedagogical model that appeared to respect and support individual human beings. Children would not be viewed as empty vessels. Further, the focus in developmental psychology on mother "love" was transformed into expectations for teachers as they became part of a previously male–dominated profession (Walkerdine, 1984). With the post-World War II concern for democracy, child–centeredness evolved as synonymous with the creation of a democratic, free society. As the key theorist influencing "progressive" educational practices of the 1960s and 1970s, Jean Piaget (however unconsciously) promoted the belief in teaching that is based on child interests, needs, and the understanding of child development (Burman, 1994). Piaget's description of stages of progress and cognitive structures provided advocates for child–centered instruction with the "scientific" information concerning the child that could be used to foster child–centeredness without the necessity of real collaboration or getting to know individual people. Further, those children with whom one came into contact could thus be expected to function and think in particular ways.

Central Tenets of Child–Centered Pedagogy

Erica Burman (1994) discusses five central tenets of child–centeredness: readiness, choice, needs, play, and discovery. Concerned with cognitive, social, and emotional development, readiness focuses on the maturity and experience base that naturally determines when a child is prepared to learn. Choice implies that the individual child is in charge by controlling the content (his/her interests) and timing of learning. As discussed in Chapter 2, childhood is constructed as a period in which the individual has basic fundamental needs that if not met will result in pathology; child–centeredness is viewed as a natural way of meeting those needs. Play is child–centered learning in action as children voluntarily self–direct their own activities. Discovery is the personal, individual experience of learning. At first glance, these components of child–centered pedagogy would appear sound and grounded in genuine concern for people. Critical analysis of these central tenets, however, reveals an ideology that is not respectful of all human beings and does not necessarily provide human support.

Readiness as Adult Privilege

Child–centered pedagogy is posited as the teaching method that provides the child with a natural opportunity to learn as she/he is ready. Whether maturationist, environmentalist, or a composite of the two, readiness is defined as the preparedness for learning that is located within the child (Graue, 1993). The concept of readiness emerged both from developmental psychology and a psychological perspective that combined biology and environment. "Readiness is a function of both general cognitive maturity and of particularized learning experience" (Ausubel, 1963, p. 30). The assumptions are consistent with those that have already been discussed in Chapter 3 regarding developmental psychology. Readiness assumes progressive, predetermined, linear change and, through the concept of maturity, privileges adult functioning and control. But, what of other assumptions that ground the construction of readiness?

First, readiness is assumed to be located within the child, resulting in a perspective in which the child (or his/her family) is blamed when progress does not occur. The child is labeled as immature or lacking in experience. The societal context and the possibility that readiness is a social construction (Graue, 1993) are denied. Second, application of the notion of readiness implies that there are those who can be categorized (by adults) as not ready. The concept becomes a gatekeeping mechanism imposed by those who are older. Third, readiness is used to mask ambiguity and behaviors that adults do not understand. Finally, the concept of readiness serves as the foundation for surveillance of children by adults. Constructed within the context of child development, children are observed and monitored to determine what they are ready for and the needed experiences that could lead to more advanced forms of readiness. Within child–centered pedagogy, younger human beings are more observed than ever before (Rose, 1985). Adults have legitimized the power of surveillance as pedagogy, without the need for permission or critique. One need only ask the question: "Would adults agree to be observed for hours every day of their lives?"

Choice as the Illusion of Individual, Self-Governance

Key within the child–centered discourse are notions of autonomy and democracy (Burman, 1994). Child–centeredness is promoted as anti–authoritarian and facilitating individual choice and self-governance. But, what of the assumptions underlying this educational belief in freedom offered through child–centeredness? What is meant by choice? Who is involved in the construction of choice? Is the purpose of self-governance to provide more freedom for all involved?

One must recognitize that freedom and democracy carry a variety of meanings for readers in different contexts. The traditional North American argument is that freedom is action based on individual choice as long as other individuals are not harmed. The individual is viewed as independent from the surrounding world, open to infinite possibilities, and possessing the resources to follow through with choices. This dominant view of freedom denies the diverse and limited contexts in which individuals live even within one democratic society. Additionally, tension is created between the construction of the individual as self-reliant, independent, and responsible and the construction of the individual as self–interested, competitive, and self–centered. Further tensions result as diverse cultural perspectives emerge that embed the individual within different cultures. Finally, when the individual is the unit of choice (the only site of freedom), gender, class, and cultural inequities are denied. These issues regarding choice are not simply applicable to those who are younger, but also apply to those who are older.

We need only to observe in teacher education discussions of discipline or early childhood classroom constructions of rules to get a feel for the real meaning of choice for children. The response usually represents a narrow range of choices:

Children are more likely to follow the rules that they construct themselves. They create harsher discipline than we do.
The teacher often guides the children to construct his/her rules.
At this learning center, a child can choose to play a game, listen to a tape, or write a story.
The child can be given the choice of staying with the group for story time or sitting in his seat and working quietly.
When the child feels that she can cooperate with the group, she can "choose" to join us.
You can use voting in the classroom as a democratic tool of choice.

Psychologists and early childhood educators have for years discussed constructing democratic environments in which children are given choices. For example, Hymes wrote "In this country you don't have to be twenty-one to vote ... in families. Children cast their votes from eighteen months on, and their vote is counted (1955, p 110). Hymes did not, however, advocate for the abolition of voting age requirements in the public world outside the family.

Choice for children is actually an illusion. Although, children can be given choice within the privacy (and control) of their homes or within the pretend environment of the school, through the use of materials and experiences, adults actually control the choices that surround children and the capacity for follow–through when choices are made. Choice for children is an illusion.

The assumption that underlies self–governance is a belief concerning how children are most likely to be regulated. Rousseau's belief in covert control (as discussed in Chapter 5) illustrates the reasoning behind attempts to create self–governed citizens and children. People are expected to consciously resist overt authority. Yet, when the environment is structured so that the participants believe that decisions are based on their own deliberations, covert control is established. The will is imprisoned through the pretence of freedom. As Burman explains, "Child–centered approaches are still associated with those preoccupations with social control and regulation, only with self–regulation regarded as more effective than overt coercion precisely because it gives the impression of freedom and choice" (1994, p. 174).

Needs as Natural Authority

Central to the notion of child–centered pedagogy is the belief that one major purpose of education is to "meet the needs" of the child. Further, child–centeredness is constructed as the ideal way to meet those needs because the child becomes the focus of instruction, the center of observation, the foundation for decisions. The child may even determine his/her own needs. This discourse is problematic, to say the least, and potentially disastrous. First, the notion that children are allowed to display their own needs can be called into question given the above discussion regarding choice in child–centeredness. Within our present ideology, children can only display needs that we will recognize because they fit into our constructions of childhood. In Chapter 2, we have discussed how the discourse of the universally needy child can actually mask the knowledge, skills, and strengths of younger human beings. Further, the notion that child needs can be identified oversimplifies human society and privileges those who are older (and sometimes those who are labeled "expert") with authority over others.

We can find multiple examples of our discourse regarding child needs:

We stress this ... need of the child to be accepted as a unique individual, or, if the parents ...will not accord that acceptance, the need to be protected and reinforced against the destructive, warping influence of those parental biases (Frank, 1938, p. 356).

The child, for the full and harmonious development of his personality, needs love and understanding (United Nations, 1959, p. 178).

The need for love and security is met by the child experiencing from birth onwards a stable, continuous, loving and mutually enjoyable relationship with his mother (Kellmer-Pringle, 1975, p. 97).

Young children need to be with adults who are interested and interesting ... they need to have natural objects and artifacts to handle and explore (House of Commons, 1988, paragraph 5.1).
Appeal to children's needs to communicate (DeVries & Zan, 1994, p. 256).
You (the child) need to sit down now. You need to be alone for a while (Silin, 1995, p. 133).

The discourse of children's needs masks our uncertainties and our disagreements about what is best for human beings, but more importantly it is used to construct a form of natural authority used to support personal, political, and power agendas. The needy label constructs authority for those who identify and address needs (Woodhead, 1990). Needy children are created as helpless and passive. The construction of natural needs, whether sentimentalized in notions of love, security, and experience (Kellmer-Pringle, 1975) or psychologized in notions of social, emotional, or cognitive development, results in a form of scientific authority in which needs are not questioned. "Need" is interpreted as a characteristic that is intrinsic to children, a scientific truth. The discourse legitimizes our surveillance and judgment of children, to determine needs, and our control of children, to respond to those needs.

Further, the discourse of need perpetuates particular ideologies without benefit of critique. The cultural context of adult value–positions are ignored. The construction of need as "fact" denies the value context within which the needs are created. Global inferences are made about children without regard to history, context or political agendas (Woodhead, 1990). As examples, Wadsworth (1986) has posited that different attitudes toward divorce in different cultural contexts produce different reactions in children. Trauma may result in one context but not in another. Children are constructed as needing "right values" in the discourse of the 1990s. Not only is this discourse deterministic, but it is a veiled attempt to control both children and particular groups of adults. Using child needs as a central tenet, child–centered pedagogy is constructed as without ideological bias, as grounded in natural science, and as more appropriate than other teaching methods. A teaching truth is created without critique.

Play as Cultural Artifact

Virtually all early childhood educators (and many others) espouse play as a sacred right of childhood, as the way in which young human beings learn, as a major avenue through which children learn to be happy, mentally healthy human beings. The history of play as a psychological construct can be traced in the work of Axline, Freud, and Erikson, who suggested that play provides a healing outlet for emotions. Consistent with the focus on universal developmental progress, Parten (1932) constructed the stages of "playing with others" as advancing from momentary interest to the creation of a common play goal. Various psychological perspectives have associated play with such constructs as exploration and creativity (Kelly-Byrne, 1989). Again, the work of Piaget provided a "scientific" knowledge base for those advocating play as the child's work. Both stages of play development and cognitive structures have been described. Play has been constructed as the avenue for psychological development in the early years. Play is considered a central tenet of child–centered pedagogy because it has been constructed as what is "natural" for children. The "naturalness" of play results in the perfect construct for use in education at home and school, intervention, evaluation, and therapy. We allow children to play; we encourage them; at times, we even teach them to play. We judge whether the type of play is normal for a particular age group, productive of cognitive or social growth, advanced, beneficial or even therapeutic.

Created as a natural right of childhood, we have not questioned this "perfect" construct. Is play the ideal construct that we have created? Again, based on the discussions of previous chapters (predominantly Chapter 3), one could critique play as a psychological construct that, when described in stages or cognitive structures, limits possibilities in ways that are similar to the notion of child development. Our constructions of play assume linearity, universal human behavior, unidirectional progress, and standards of normalcy. By now, these assumptions should be obvious. However, play can be further problematized as the artifact of a particular culture whose beliefs about younger human beings are not necessarily applicable to all.

In his historical analysis of European games and pastimes, Aries (1962) has described play as societal activity that involved people of all ages. "Toys," including dolls, were first created as replicas of the real world and most often placed in tombs. Children most likely played with these toys, but the origins were adult ritual, pleasure, and amusement. Everyone appeared to enjoy the miniature replication of daily life. By 1600, specialty toys were created for infants, but this differentiation did not extend beyond the age of three or four. Younger human beings tended to play the same games as adults, whether with adults or other children. Dolls were most often given as gifts to women as models for fashion. In the 1700s, puppet shows were the most popular form of entertainment in Paris for all ages. Very young children played games like tennis and hockey that are today considered only appropriate for adolescents or adults. Conversely, adults played games that are today considered only appropriate for children. Both adults and children took part in society's games and folk pastimes, such as festivals. When play was differentiated, it occurred along socioeconomic lines, at times placing children, females, and the poor into the same subservient, dependent group (Hoyles, 1979). In past generations of European society, people of all ages played.

Studies in diverse cultures demonstrate the ways in which play is a Euro-American middle–class construct, an artifact of a particular view of the world. For example, Piaget described play as a major contributor to the process of assimilation. From this perspective, infants are viewed as exploring the world by using objects and repeating actions over and over. During the first two years of life, this sensorimotor play is considered essential. Shirley Brice Heath's (1983) classic ethnographic work in the rural Carolinas contradicts this view of play. She describes young children in a particular cultural community as having very little opportunity to interact with objects in the physical world. The young children in Heath's study were held and cuddled constantly by other human beings. The notion of sensorimotor exploration does not seem appropriate for the context that she describes.

Dominant constructions of play have ignored the voices of people of color. For example, in the book *He Said-She Said*, Margorie Goodwin (1990) demonstrates how Black children prefer forms of play that are verbal, rather than object oriented. Yet, verbal play is not part of the accepted view of play. Verbalization is constructed as too abstract unless tied concretely to play behavior. Further, when play with words involves objectionable language, adults attempt to censor the play. We begin to realize that play is not only a cultural artifact, but an artifact to be controlled and even suppressed when dominant forms are not exhibited.

Symbolic play, also proposed by Piaget, is another construct that has been described as if existent regardless of time, culture, or context. For example, the activity of Yup'ik Eskimo girls as they conduct story-knifing (deMarrais, Nelson & Baker, 1994) displays symbolic overtones but does not fit the dominant construction of symbolic play. The girls spend hours telling stories by drawing symbols in riverbank mud palettes. The story-knifing activities build on the cooperation and consensus that are part of traditional Eskimo culture. Although somewhat symbolic, these stories would mean nothing independent of the cultural context (Vaalsiner, 1989). So too with the context in which Piaget's children found themselves. They functioned in ways that fit the European culture of the times. The notion that children all over the world display a form of Piagetian symbolic play not only denies context but creates dangerous and inappropriate expectations for people living in a variety of life situations.

The psychologization of play has resulted in the belief that young children are incapable of playing games with rules. Games have been constructed as different than play and most appropriate for those who are older. Yet, just as Aries has demonstrated the involvement of very young children in adult games during past centuries, perspectives from other cultures do not necessarily lead to an ordered understanding of games nor to the separation of games as a higher–level play activity. The Grand Valley Dani in Indonesia (Heider, 1977) illustrate the cultural embeddedness of the construction of games. The Dani are farmers who do not believe in competition or keeping records, like scores, that would lead to winners or losers. Indonesian teachers introduced the Dani to the game called Flip the Stick that requires that the batter use a long stick to flip a short one as many times as possible before other players catch the stick. The batter with the most points wins. Years after the game was introduced to the Dani children, observers found that an indigenous form of the game had replaced the original version. Rules no longer involved competition, keeping score, or winners and losers. Value assumptions that do not necessarily apply to all human beings underlie the western concept of games.

Additionally, underlying the cultural construction of play is the distinction between play and work. Play rhetoric is consistently associated with pleasure, with voluntary activity under the individual's own control. Work is that which is under the control of another (King, 1992). The play/work separation can be traced to a long–held practice of marginalizing the activities of children and the poor (Hoyles, 1979). Further, Kelly-Byrne (1989) associates this idealized construction of play with the naturalized version of childhood that dominates the western world. Since childhood is a time to prepare for and learn about life, it is constructed as the time in which play is legitimate (Bloch, 1986). However, King (1987) found that children generally view kindergarten activities such as listening to stories and painting as work, not play. Although they enjoyed the activities, children seem to recognize the role of context and do not create the same types of distinctions as adults. Espousing "play as the young child's work", adults actually construct environments for children that reflect their constructions of what is appropriate through play, their own culturally created agendas for controlling children.

This play/work distinction is not only applied to children, but dominates western industrialized perspectives. The modern separation of the public and the private as illustrated by the distinction between the world of work and the safety of the home is an example. Hunt and Frankenberg (1990) have examined Disney (Disneyland and Disney World) as a modern–day concrete representation of the separation of play and work. The illusion of play is so complete that even those workers who spend 8–10 hours each day on their feet in the hot sun are to appear as if all is right with the world and everyone is having fun. Disney further illustrates the western construction of play as exclusive and requiring particular proper behaviors. For example, just as middle–class Americans and Europeans are concerned with buying the appropriate toys with which their children will play, the price of admission into Disney parks excludes those who are poor. Not only is the distinction between work and play reinforced, but a dominant view of play is perpetuated.

Around the world, play and work are not constructed as dichotomous concepts. For example, most studies with African children reveal a mix of activities (Bloch & Adler, 1994). Lancy (1984) found that children observe as apprentices and pretend learning behaviors as they watch a blacksmith and then practice by beating on rocks. As part of the work of Bloch and Adler, one man describes practicing herding with a stick. In some contexts, we would not even find language that would create the two as separate or distinct.

Finally, although play is considered the "young child's work" by western educators, psychologists, and even some parents, the freedom that is implied for young children within the construction of play is a false liberty. Adults have created play as "good" and "bad," "appropriate" and "inappropriate." Children are judged as exhibiting productive, beneficial, or therapeutic play. Children are judged as exhibiting aggressive, disruptive, or dangerous play. Although the discourse may be to allow children to explore and make sence of their world, when the play behavior does not suit those who are in control, the voluntary activity is no longer allowed. Adults are really in control.

Play is clearly a cultural artifact, representing a view of the world in which (1) stages of progress are predetermined for human beings, (2) learning is viewed as exploration with objects, and (3) the way human beings function can be dichotomized into oppositional behaviors. Child–centered pedagogy and play as a central tenet within educational practice have been created in a particular culture with particular values and biases. Applying the notion of play to all peoples in all contexts denies the multiple value structures, knowledges, and views of the world which are created by people in diverse contexts.

Discovery as Privileging Monocultural Knowledge

Child–centeredness assumes isolated individuals (Burman, 1994) with socioeconomic privilege and a shared value base (Freire & Macedo, 1987; Delpit, 1993). The concept of discovery assumes the existence of a universal knowledge base that all human beings value and discover equally, similarity of experiences, and access to materials that is equitable. A variety of scholars (Banks, 1993; Lincoln & Guba, 1985) have questioned the notion of a universal knowledge base, proposing that knowledge is socially constructed by different groups in different historical, political, and value contexts. Different knowledges are created and valued by different cultures through diverse life experiences. Knowledge is therefore a cultural artifact, replete with codes and rules for understanding. The experiences that generate knowledge and the materials used for the attainment of information vary depending on the culture(s) involved, the knowledge(s) constructed and chosen as important, and the societal contexts within which learning occurs.

Lisa Delpit (1993) has demonstrated how child–centered pedagogy, and the resultant focus on discovery learning, privileges knowledge considered important by the upper and middle class. She proposes the existence of a "culture of power" (p. 121). This culture includes the knowledge, communication methods, strategies for the construction of self, and methods of personal presentation that are valued by those in power. Success in school, the work place, and society in general is dependent on acquiring the knowledge that is created by this culture of power. Children from the upper and middle class are more successful in school because their home and school both represent the culture of power. These children can "discover" knowledge of a particular type because most of their life experiences are constructed by the culture of power.

"Children from other kinds of families operate with perfectly wonderful and viable cultures but not cultures that carry the codes or rules of power" (Delpit, 1993, p. 122). Those who are not part of the culture of power can most easily be successful if explicitly told the rules. Delpit uses the example of her work in the villages of Papua New Guinea. Over a lifetime of experiences, she might be expected to discover the culture. As an outsider, however, life was easier when she was directly informed of cultural expectations. Children from diverse cultural backgrounds who are placed in school environments and expected to discover the knowledge and rules of the culture of power are immediately put at a disadvantage. Recognizing that skills–based, direct–instruction approaches treat minority children as if they are without culture and deny the child's expertise in his/her own life, Delpit does not propose a full–scale use of direct–teaching methodologies. She does, however, advocate for methods that reveal cultural expectations to children, that yield greater cross–cultural communication, and that address issues of power. If we focus solely on discovery learning through child–centered pedagogy, we are functioning with a monocultural view of learning.

Finally, discovery orientations promote middle–class, liberal goals that include the development of autonomy and materialistic forms of learning. Middle class children may be free to develop an independence through which they resist standardization by outside forces, because they are already members of the culture of power. The autonomous behaviors of most middle–class individuals are not likely to create revolutionary challenges to the status quo. Those from lower socioeconomic backgrounds or other cultural contexts, or both, may however, function in entirely different ways. They may work as collaborators, by constructing self as contributing to a group, or with goals that are not consistent with notions of autonomy. Focusing on discovery learning as universal condemns diverse goals for and methods of learning to the margin of human functioning.

Discovery learning has also generally implied an environment with a variety of materials. Whether using scientific experiences, playing with toys, or exploring learning centers, a three–dimensional concrete educational environment is assumed. The availability of money for particular types of materials is implied. Even those concrete objects that are available in some locations of the real world (e.g., rocks, soil, leaves) are only superficially included. For example, a teacher education researcher in India recently praised the progress that was being made in a project in which teachers were beginning to create an environment that was more colorful and used learning centers for young children. Indian knowledge of children is being denied in the rush to create a discovery environment that is "good" by western standards. Universally imposing discovery oriented, child–centered pedagogy on all children not only places everyone in a position in which success is dependent on the availability of money for materials, but colonizes classrooms all over the world to be constructed in ways that are consistent with western middle class (and capitalist) values.

Reproducing Dominant Perspectives

The reproduction and reinforcement of the cultural knowledge of particular power groups is perhaps the major problem with child–centered pedagogy as the methodological doctrine of early childhood education. Dominant views are reproduced in at least three ways: (1) in forms of pedagogical determinism that favor middle–class views of education, (2) in the perpetuation of the masculine image as the most advanced, ideal goal of educational pursuits, and (3) in descriptions of particular forms of language as universal and necessary for human growth.

Pedagogical Determinism
When any teaching method is marketed as the best or most appropriate for a particular group of people, the assumption is that there are universal truths that are discoverable concerning teaching and that the "right" method predetermines outcomes. This pedagogical determinism is consistent with a positivist view that would scientifically reveal human truth. When, however, science (and the fields that lay claim to science such as developmental psychology) is conceived as human construction, teaching methodologies can also be understood as historically, socially, and politically grounded. Both skills–based instruction and child–centered pedagogy are understood as human constructions, emerging from

particular contexts. Any teaching method is understood as culturally bound, laden with human bias, based on particular forms of knowledge, and potentially dangerous for those whose cultural values are different from those imposed by the method. Grounded in psychological perspectives of the world and in veiled attempts to regulate particular groups of people, education has imposed the knowledge of power groups on those with less power. (For more information, see Chapters 4 and 5.) Particular teaching methods and forms of knowledge have been impressed on everyone as truth for all human beings. The most recent example of this pedagogical determinism in early childhood education is the construction of Developmentally Appropriate Practice or DAP (Bredekamp, 1987).

A set of position statements (DAP) published by the National Association for the Education of Young Children has prescribed best teaching practices as dominated by child–centered pedagogy. DAP has been and continues to be disseminated all over the world as the guide for education of young children. After some criticism regarding cultural responsiveness, the documents are currently under revision. However, with or without revision, the statements and the actions generated represent an extreme form of pedagogical determinism. First, the child is objectified, created as the Other, and presented as a universal. However diversely children are described, the assumption that method can be prescribed creates a universal child. This assumption is obvious within the title of the documents in the use of the term "appropriate," the methods that best fit the universal child. Further, the notion of appropriateness perpetuates the modernist discourse of oppositional thought; adult/child, right/wrong, white/black, male/female, appropriate/inappropriate.

Second, DAP privileges forms of logical thought that dominate developmental psychology. This knowledge is represented as truth, whether in reference to child development research with children, active learning, or appropriate teaching methods. DAP is prescribed as the child–centered pedagogy that should be used with all children. The diverse knowledges and ways of learning that are demonstrated by different cultural groups in the United States and around the world are silenced. Those who have learned and been happy throughout their lives without child–centered pedagogy are ignored. (See O'Loughlin, 1992 for an in–depth discussion.)

Finally, DAP has been constructed as an official knowledge (Apple, 1993, 1996; Lubeck, 1994). Those who disagree with or question that knowledge are placed in the margin. Learning is only recognized and legitimized if it falls within what is conceptualized as developmentally appropriate. The pedagogical determinism is most certainly complete.

Masculine Images

As Walkerdine (1988) has clearly demonstrated, "the quintessential developing child is a boy" (Burman, 1994, p. 157). Based on child development, child–centered pedagogy positions the child as pioneer, explorer, constructor, and developer of independence, a stereotypic masculine image. Power and autonomy are promoted. Mothers and teachers are even told to allow children to make a mess, to explore so that they will know they are in control. Piaget's theory is used as scientific legitimation for the masculinized construction of the individual as isolated and separate from the world. In a child–centered environment, the individual person is expected to progress toward the higher point of intellectual development — advanced scientific logic. Forms of knowledge that are constructed through gendered female experiences or nontraditional female/male knowledges are placed in the margin. Female children, although ultimately expected to be cooperative and subservient, are given the contradictory image that independence and exploration are to be rewarded.

Child–centeredness covertly places children under increased patriarchal control, denying their roles as agents in the world. As demonstrated previously, advocates who are against child labor have insisted that children be protected from the public world and that they should have a time to play and be free. Removing children from the world of work denies the contributions that they have made and can make in various societies. In the United States, those who are between 9– and 15– or 16– years–of–age were once an integral part of the functioning of this society. Even those who were younger often cared for infants. Many of those children now either have nothing to do, base their sense of self on arbitrary school grades, serve as sports entertainment for their parents, or join gangs.

In other countries, the dangers that are constructed by patriarchal child–centeredness may be even worse. The family may depend on all members working (including those who are younger) for food and survival. Without work, and labeled unknowing and helpless, children have even been killed by those in power who have been designated as protectors (Burman, 1994).

Without critique, child–centeredness fosters patriarchy and a construction of childhood with less power and requiring regulation.

Language Universals

Whether in the home or school, child–centered pedagogy is closely associated with particular ways of communicating with children. Most of us as teacher educators or "experts" who would give advice to parents have suggested:

> *Be available to respond to the child's questions.*
> *Talk as you work so the child knows what's happening.*
> *Ask the child questions.*
> *Look at picture books and talk about what you see.*
> *Sing songs, say rhymes, and play counting games.*

Child–centered language forms are dominated by the discourse of maternal sensitivity, the responsive, positive style used by the middle class as they attend to child behavior (Burman, 1994; Woollett & Phoenix, 1991). Created out of the psychological stereotype of "good mothering" (Pine, 1992), child–oriented language has been constructed as conversation that is sensitive as opposed to direct, intrusive, and regulatory (Nelson, 1973; McDonald & Pien, 1982). The cultural embeddedness of psycholinguistic practice and the impact of imposing a particular practice on everyone is not recognized.

The works of Bambi Schieffelin (1990), Elinor Ochs (1988), and Shirley Brice Health (1983) have all demonstrated that the use of language by children and adults reflects the beliefs of the culture in which the individual learns to function. "All societies do not rely on the very same set of language–socialising procedures" (Ochs, 1986, p. 6). Privileging one set of procedures over another privileges one group over another. For example, "a mother who 'orders her child around' (Nelson, 1973, p. 68) is seen as being 'intrusive', whereas a mother who insists on her child answering a long series of 'What's that?' questions is not" (Pine, 1992, p. 5). Even when cross–cultural research has revealed child–centered speech, the participants who represented diverse cultures were almost exclusively educated and middle class (Burman, 1994), the group that is most privileged through child–centeredness. Children around the world learn to talk both with and without a child–centered speech code.

In addition to creating false liberties and covert regulation of children (as discussed previously in this chapter), the universalization of child–centered speech constructs a position in which women as mothers and teachers are controlled. To be responsive to children, the female is expected to either ignore all other responsibilities (e.g., household work, community activities, family financial support) or convert them into educational possibilities for children. Women are virtually told how to act throughout the day. Again, the dominant focus on the "good mother" results in a narrow construction of female identity as tied to younger human beings. Women and children are both regulated, expected to live their lives within a dominant construction that is child–centeredness.

Challenging Child-Centeredness

As some have read this chapter, I can imagine at least some of the comments and questions that may be generated:

These ideas are ridiculous; I place children first and that's what's important.
Do we eliminate child–centeredness because its an evil perpetuated by those in power, by those who would have their own culture dominate?

Child-centeredness is not "the product of some repressive superpower hell-bent on keeping people in their place." Child-centeredness is actually a "reproduction of ourselves" (Walkerdine, 1984, p. 194). Liberals, feminists, radicals and any others who would place younger human beings first have genuinely believed that child–centeredness is liberatory. Since child–centered pedagogy is either consistent with our own experiences or seems to provide an alternative to overt oppression, we have embraced its tenets. Yet without critique, we have denied the complexity of education, the historical and political embeddedness of educational ideology, our biases toward our own lived experiences, and the covert assumptions that ground child–centeredness. We cannot ignore the challenges:

(1)   Within the construction of child–centeredness, adults have legitimized the power of surveillance and judgment over children. The rights and privacy of younger human beings are denied in the

name of educational judgment and adult supremacy over education.

(2)   Child–centeredness constructs the illusion that children in educational environments have choice when actually the "will" is imprisoned through the pretense of freedom. Self–regulation is used as more effective than overt control, which may actually be more easily resisted.

(3)   The discourse of need, a central tenet of child–centered pedagogy, perpetuates particular deterministic ideologies and is not recognized as a cultural construction. Need is used to construct a form of natural authority supporting political and power agendas. Using the authority created through the concept of need, child–centeredness is constructed as the truth.

(4)   Child–centered pedagogy and play, as central tenets within educational practice, have been created in a particular culture with particular values and biases. Applying the notion of play to all peoples in all situations denies the multiple value structures, knowledges, and views of the world which are created by people in diverse contexts.

(5)   Universally imposing discovery and child-centered pedagogy on all children not only places everyone in a position in which success is dependent on the availability of money and materials, but colonizes classrooms all over the world to be constructed in ways that are consistent with western middle–class values.

(6)   Child–centeredness is the reproduction of the cultural capital of particular power groups — for examples, those who believe that child development is truth, those who would perpetuate gendered masculine images, or those who construct their own forms of communication as superior to others. This power is not always exercised consciously, but is imposed on others regardless.

Child–centered pedagogy and play–based instruction would appear to be the ideal forms of education that would place younger human beings at the forefront. However, critique reveals that this is not the case. Hidden constructions of power may be even more oppressive than overt displays of force. Further, imposing child–centered pedagogy on all human beings simply perpetuates deterministic, universal–truth orientations.

Chapter VII

Disciplining Women and Children

Women, through our work as mothers, as students, and as teachers, have contributed our labor and our children to institutional and social organizations that have extended our own subordination and contradicted our own experiences of nurturance.

Grumet, 1988, p 45

Early childhood educators continue to advocate for recognition and respect for younger human beings and the work of those who share their lives. We all recognize that the general public and even those in other fields of education at times refer to work with young children as "babysitting" or "play."

How difficult can it be to play with or read stories to children?

This patriarchal assumption is most recently publicly stated in President George Bush's goals for the year 2000 in which all children were to start school "ready to learn" (Boyer, 1993, p. 54), as if the lives of younger human beings do not involve thought or learning before they enter school. Additionally, the human interactions between children and those around them (whether mothers or teachers) are assumed to be of less significance than our expectations for rationalized, controlled schooling. This clear lack of respect for both children and those who work with them has led all educators, and those who work with young children in particular, to fight for the professionalization of the field. This fight has focused on improving educational opportunities for children and generating respect for teachers, a clearly warranted agenda. However, the struggle has not always been with the recognition that professionalism is a double–edged sword that (1) could lead to a strengthening of position and increased respect, but (2) has more often resulted in increased domination by those in power.

The argument could be made that advocacy for the field of early childhood education as a profession is a separate issue from the creation of teaching in general as a profession. After all, early education and elementary education (not to mention secondary) have clearly different histories and societal institutions. As has been discussed previously, early education is grounded in psychological research and dominated by child development perspectives (Bloch, 1992). The institutions most closely associated with early childhood education are day care, nursery schools, and kindergartens. These institutions were historically tied to schools of social work or child development programs, rather than colleges of education. As Takanishi (1982) has demonstrated, researchers devoted their time to child development (and the teaching of it), not to issues of teacher education. While not always obvious in other fields of education, early childhood education has clearly been dominated by theories and research in psychology as the professional knowledge base for the field.

I would, however, argue that early childhood education is bound to other fields of education since all have emerged from within a patriarchal societal structure in which teaching came to be viewed as women's work and science was constructed as the authority for action. Early and recent attempts to create education as a profession are grounded within this patriarchal structure that privileges scientific judgment and hierarchical relationships. Further, professional language is used as a mechanism for control, and sites of power are created in the promotion of truth–bearing knowledge bases. Rational, hierarchical theories have been used to construct power roles, male over female, European over non–European, adult over child. The professionalization of education (whether early childhood or other forms of education) has resulted in the fostering of this same patriarchal power over both women and children. The discourses and actions associated with professional institutions and practice have generated disciplinary and regulatory powers over teachers (who are mostly women) and children (Foucault, 1978; see also Chapter 4). Standards have been created through which individuals judge and limit themselves, through which they construct a desire to be "good," "normal," or both.

The purpose of this chapter is to analyze the notion of education, and particularly early childhood education, as a profession. The ways in which the discourses of professionalism support the sexism, racism, and class division found in the patriarchal status quo and create disciplinary powers over women and regulatory power over children are examined. To problematize the concept of professionalism, we must first call attention to the patriarchal hegemony that has structured western society, resulting in gendered mental constructs that dominate but are largely invisible in our interpretations of the world (Lerner, 1993).

Patriarchy and Education

Gerda Lerner (1993; 1986) has located the creation of patriarchy before the construction of western civilization. Patriarchal perspectives have so dominated the west that male control over females is accepted as universal for societal order. Unstated gender assumptions are so prevalent in western mental constructs as to be invisible. Males are considered the norm, females the abnormal. Males are whole, powerful, and rational; females are unfinished, dependent, and emotional. Lerner further illustrates how the construction of western perspectives around male dominance over females led to other forms of dominance — for example, slavery. Patriarchy has resulted in societies of hierarchical domination based on sex, race, social class, age, and any other forms of difference that might be generated.

Patriarchal societies function with several basic assumptions: Males and females are essentially, biologically, and socially different. Because males are the strongest and most rational, they are naturally superior to females and designed as those who would be the political citizens. The male function is to explain, order, and control the world. The female function is nurturance and reproduction. Although both functions are essential to human survival, the male function transcends the material universe. The female function is more basic, as with children and more "savage" peoples. Males are inherently given the right to control female sexuality and are the mediators between God and females (Lerner, 1993). These unprovable laws have been acted upon in a variety of ways in different cultural contexts and time periods. For example, in an age in which one man ruling another was called to question, Aristotle used gender to justify slavery. He reasoned that some are born to rule and others to be ruled. "The male is by nature superior, and the female inferior; and the one rules and the other is ruled; this principle, of necessity extends to all mankind" (Aristotle, 1941, p. 1132).

When the constructors of the Declaration of Independence in the United States declared that "all men are created equal," an uneasiness with slavery was expressed by many. Although the right to participatory citizenship took many years to accomplish (and many of us would agree that equity has not yet been achieved), there was at least the recognition of the issue. The founding "fathers" did not debate even liberty, happiness, or rights for women. Lerner (1993) illustrates the lack of consciousness regarding women in the response of John Adams to his wife Abigail who had requested that he plan for the protection of women against the tyranny of their husbands. He could not but laugh that another tribe (and compared women to children, Indians, and Negroes) who already possessed some power had "grown discontented." Chastising her for notions that if acted upon would lead to disorder, he stated "we know better than to repeal our Masculine systems" (Butterfield, Friedlaender, & Kline, 1975, p. 123). Lerner reminds the reader that throughout the history of the west, "men's power to define" has been the foundation for the meaning of social order (p. 9).

Modern philosophical theories and scientific thought perpetuate patriarchal assumptions and are constructed in ways that deny power to anyone who disputes them. "Women have been defined out and marginalized in every philosophical system and have therefore had to struggle not only against exclusion but against a content which defines them as subhuman and deviant" (Lerner, 1993, p. 5). For example, when the child–study movement began, women were seen as sentimental, lacking the objectivity necessary for rational child observation (Burman, 1994). In previous chapters, I have discussed the construction by "objective" males of a psychology based on rational, hierarchical theories. Women have invariably been either defined out or ignored. Psychological technologies of measurement and comparison further support the construction of patriarchal systems in which one group dominates another through the imposition of logical thought over subjugated forms of knowledge, objectivity over subjectivity, truth over ambiguity, or expert over novice.

Defining Education as Woman's Work

In the United States, and many other countries, teaching has both promoted patriarchy and been created by patriarchal assumptions. Women did not simply take up teaching, but "teaching took up women" (Grumet, 1988, p. 33). The story is most easily understood by examining changes that occurred with the modern age. Before the industrial era of the nineteenth century, the household was the productive unit in society. Agriculture, food preparation, and the production of required commodities (e.g., cloth, furniture) were functions of the domestic unit. Both females and males contributed. Industrialization resulted in a separation between the private and public. Labor positions were created by the invention of machinery and the construction of factories, resulting in greater job opportunities most often open to males. With increased opportunities, males were no longer interested in teaching. Living within the limits placed on them by patriarchal assumptions, women had few work opportunities outside the home. As males chose to leave teaching, women took it up as an additional option for employment to be added to domestic service and textile mill work.

Although providing women with an additional employment possibility, teaching for women was always supported with the belief that salaries could and should be less for females. In 1855, Horace Mann (Morain, 1980) used frugality as his rationale for the employment of women in the Iowa system. Catharine Beecher, in her request to Congress in 1853 for the support of national education, legitimated the possibility through the expectation of lower salaries for female teachers. "Women can afford to teach for one half, or even less the salary which men would ask, because the female teacher has only to sustain herself; she does not look forward to the duty of supporting a family" (Sklar, 1973, p. 182).

As women were constructed as the moral foundation of the family and the instrument whose identity is inextricably tied to the child, teaching was declared the natural responsibility of women. In the name of motherhood, women were claimed to be the best suited to educate children. Beecher maintained that domesticity, self-sacrifice, and submissiveness were the morally superior female characteristics that were needed in education. She was joined by others in the construction of gendered roles as tied to education. As examples, Elizabeth Peabody supported Froebel's view of women as those who ultimately submit their will for the good of the child. Literature of the day described women's virtues as patience, silence, and self-denial, while their vices were described as pride, willfulness, and activity. Patriarchal authority was established; women were perpetuated as having particular submissive characteristics that were unquestionably tied to children (Grumet, 1988). Teaching took up and controlled women. (For discussions of the societal and personal context in which Catharine Beecher lived, see Sklar, 1973 and Munro, 1996).

Consistent with a patriarchal perspective, women's jobs have historically been proletarianized. A sexual division of labor has placed women in positions with lower pay, less autonomy, and increased control. As women have become the majority employed in a field, outside control over content and practice has emerged. For example, clerical work was originally a path to managerial positions and was dominated in numbers by males. As females became the majority holding clerical positions, wages were lowered and the work was deskilled and placed under control from outside (Apple, 1987). Teaching is another excellent example of decreasing wages and increasing proletarianization. To illustrate, as women entered teaching, they were paid approximately two-thirds of a male salary in England and one-half to one-third a male salary in the United States. The proletarianization of teaching is obvious in the movements to reform education, and the creation of knowledge bases and methods for teaching accountability. This proletarianization is further illustrated in the construction of teaching as a profession.

The feminization of teaching thoroughly demonstrates patriarchal assumptions and claims to power. Women were brought into education because of proposed characteristics that were inherent in the mother–child relationship (teaching taking up women). Yet, the work of the ideal teacher would be control, the perpetuation of the social order. Teachers were to comply with the demands of school committees and boards, to yield to the control of "superiors" and to control the behavior and learning of children. The "good teacher" was and is expected to demand "order in the name of sweetness, ... citizenship in the name of silence, and asexuality in the name of manners" (Grumet, 1988, p. 44).

Delivering Children to the Patriarchy

Madeleine Grumet (1988) has examined how women in the west have been defined as agents to deliver children to the state. Based on enlightenment perspectives and compounded by the inequities of the industrial era, a class of people has emerged who view affluence as the right of advanced intellect in a rational world. This group has defined societal problems as intrinsic within characteristics of the poor. The children of the working class, immigrants, and farmers would only overcome these "dysfunctional" characteristics if the state provides substitute paternity. These children would only become part of a productive national citizenry through schooling. This schooling was and is veiled in the discourse of maternal nurturance, providing support, care, and even love for younger members of society. Yet female teachers are expected to use the rules, regulations, and language of the patriarchy. Children are defined as those who must be covertly or overtly controlled, disciplined either by internalized regulatory powers or physical constraint, and judged developmentally or scholastically, socially or emotionally.

Teachers, who are mostly women, are defined as those who are to calmly and intelligently demand that children yield to the knowledge of the patriarchy and to control those who would resist. Further, when teachers disagree with the dominant regime or when they do not succeed in controlling a child's resistance, they are taught to blame their own intellect, motivation, or effort. If that blame does not work, the personal characteristics or the life circumstance of the child are condemned. The patriarchal function of schooling is never called to question or implicated. Teaching has been created as the ultimate gendered profession, the "good female" instructing the younger members of society how to yield to and support the "male controlled" world.

Patriarchy and the Construction of Education as a Profession

The meaning of professionalism (and consequently, the construction of a profession) has changed depending on the social and political context in which it was used. According to Densmore (1987), the professions have usually required an extensive period of training and the acquisition of a particular knowledge base that is both broad and theoretical. Job privileges, such as elevated social status and financial advantage, have been most often justified based on the notion that professionals are highly skilled and offer specialized public service. Professionals have been considered those who are autonomous in the quality application of skills without supervision or outside controls. Larson (1977) has, however, pointed out that the public service and work–ethic orientations associated with professionalism are actually rooted in precapitalist histories. Under capitalism, the bases for professionalism changed, becoming the method in which particular groups distinguish themselves from others. Status as an expert and privilege over those who are not professionals appears to be the dominant ideology.

As a construct, professionalism derives social authority by laying claim to the "truth" of science and the assumption that only a particular group of individuals will learn enough to administer knowledge. Further, enlightenment and modernist beliefs in truth as existent, predetermined, and universal lead to an asocial, acultural construction of professionalism. If science yields universal truths, then the expert is politically neutral. Consistent with the patriarchal notion that particular people are to explain, order, and control the world for others, expert professionals are simply dispensing the truth to those who need it.

In addition to diversity in definition and ideology, professionalism is grounded in the complex, diverse contexts from which it emerges. Popkewitz (1994) demonstrates how professionalism is an American and British construction, "profession" being an Anglo–Saxon term. He describes professionalism as a method of private social regulation. In countries with centralized governments, professionalization appears less likely because the state controls occupational activity. In countries with less centralized government like the United States and Britain, private groups create methods of regulation. For example, as the Swedish government allows for more local control in educational decision making, Popkewitz expects professional expert groups to assume regulatory power over the standards and content of teaching. When the government centralizes power, professional groups do not appear as strong. When government is decentralized, expert groups emerge that would regulate and control.

The concept of professionalism is both illusive and contradictory. Not only does it change with context, but it promotes patriarchal perspectives, legitimizing power for particular groups and denying others any form of authority. Returning to the patriarchal assumptions described in the previous section, the concept of professionalism (1) fosters the notion that one group is superior to another, (2) allows those who are members of a profession to establish order and control over particular aspects of the lives of those who are not, (3) perpetuates the notion of human differentiation in which a dominant group establishes roles for others, and (4) allows the expert group in its infinite wisdom to speak and mediate for others. Masked within a discourse of service and work, professionalism perpetuates the status quo, creating conditions of control for those who define what it means to be professional.

Teachers as Professionals

In the United States, calls for "professionalism" emerged in two forms in the latter half of the nineteenth and early part of the twentieth centuries (Popkewitz, 1994). Predominantly male administrators and university professors called for training in the development of new disciplines and established occupational hierarchies (e.g., superintendencies) through which males could pass. Until 1914, female teachers had not been part of the middle class and were viewed as wage labor, tarnished women. As the middle–class female recognized teaching as an avenue for gaining opportunity and power, education was constructed as a profession, placing women in teaching positions to be controlled by male administrators. A language of "unification" was employed, along with discourses tied to the "good mother" and the need for "national education." Further, the professional language asserted neutrality and fairness, the language of "education for all" and "democratic opportunity." Exhibiting power or disagreeing was considered unprofessional (Ginsburg, 1987).

At the bottom of the professional ladder were females who were subjected to universalized curriculum policies, standardized hiring measures, and newly developed forms of teacher evaluation (Mattingly, 1987). Education reforms further devalued teaching as an intellectual activity, replacing moral and intellectual dynamics of pedagogy with a focus on classroom management and simplification of content. For example, early manuals on the teaching of reading were small and contained philosophical questions and student bibliographies. Much was left to teacher intellect and judgment. By 1970, reading manuals were entirely scripted, laying out entire lessons, from "what to say" to students to "where to stand in the classroom" (Popkewitz, 1994, p. 4).

Teacher training was constructed as an "applied science," an education in which future teachers would learn the information and skills of the "truth" of teaching. Teacher education was and is conceived as a technical training in which management, lesson planning, predetermined content and methodologies, and scientifically legitimized behavior was and is the focus. Teacher education was constructed as nonintellectual. This approach was consistent with medical views of women as those who would apply the information given them about children by physicians, and child–study perspectives in which women were believed to be emotional and lacking objectivity. However the language of "teacher reflection" or "decision making" might be used, teacher education has been and is practiced to promote dominant patriarchal ideologies. Those who challenge the system or critique dominant perspectives are placed in the margin.

Teacher professionalism has been recently used in arguments related to education and school improvement. Just as Thorndike argued for the control of measurement and curriculum by experts grounded in the scientific research of psychology, current reform efforts privilege the "truth" pursued and revealed through research in cognition. Professional teachers are to use particular scientifically grounded practice that promotes child development, autonomy, problem solving, and that allows for individual knowledge construction. Viewed as predominantly nurturers in a field that does not require intellectual or cognitive abilities, early childhood educators have understandably sought to gain control over and respect for work with young children. We have not, however, recognized that this psychological knowledge base is grounded in the same patriarchal assumptions from which Thorndike's work emerged. A universal cognitive truth is posited and reinforced through the construction of professionalism.

Professionalism and Gendered Identities

Walkerdine describes "identity" as the "fixing of a subject in a position" that cannot occur independently from the normative views of the world created by a particular discourse (Walkerdine, 1987, p. 119). A variety of discourse practices and regimes of truth result in multiple positions in which human beings find themselves. As teachers, the identities of women are positioned as good mothers, as gendered workers, as agents of the state, and as good daughters. Further, constructed within a discourse of professionalism, these identities are accepted as truth. We see ourselves as presocial individuals, free agents who are naturally inscribed with particular attributes, strengths, and weaknesses. Perhaps female teachers of all classes were more unified through a professional ideology, but all women remained low–status human beings whose identities were regulated by others.

Good mother. We have already discussed the construction of the good mother, the female who naturally bonds, attaches, and communicates with her child because this mother/child relationship is the "foundation" for female identity. This natural female role is expected to carry over into teaching as we display love and affection to all children, as we are expected to understand the child's thoughts and needs just as mothers can "read" the needs of their own children. But, what if the behavior of the good mother and the implied good teacher does not seem natural? Most of us have no more insight into the understanding of younger human beings than into our peers or older people. We are always guessing, constructing who we think they are. Further, are we not being very presumptuous to assume that anyone could understand another human being? Can we reduce humanity to the behaviors that others observe? Additionally, some of us do not agree with the psychological, medical, or religious constructions of the good mother. Some may believe that mothering is not the major role of females and that mothering (and teaching) can occur in multiple diverse forms. The professionalization of the good teacher as the good mother not only regulates women, but constructs deviant identities for all those who disagree.

Gendered worker. Michael Apple (1983) has illustrated the ways in which the work of education has eroded as greater numbers of females entered teaching. The labor process of teaching has changed, creating a gendered identity through intensification, deskilling, and the call for accountability. Sophisticated methods for regulating teacher resistance emerged from curriculum reform movements and included management by objectives, systematic inclusion of testing, and predetermined, prepackaged curriculum. Imposed on teachers, these methods intensified the teacher's work, constructing an overload that not only eliminated time to read educational materials but even eliminated time to go to the bathroom during the school day. We now find teachers spending their days writing lesson plans, creating learning centers and units, grading stacks of papers, covering skills, and evaluating students. When labor is so intensified, identity that is self–directed, sociable, or relaxed is lost. Teachers have actually become deskilled, accepting technical knowledge and controlled behaviors. The knowledges that would be created through their own lives, imaginations, and creativity are denied. This intensification is accepted as the content of education, as required in the construction of professional behavior.

Professionalism has been part of the struggle to win equal respect and pay for women. Further, the professions (e.g., medicine) have perpetuated a gendered and classed division of labor. One can understand why women would hope that professionalization would lead to advanced status, respect, and more pay. However, professionalism has actually fostered the patriarchal, modernist notion of control and rationality.

To be a good teacher, I must be a good decision maker. I must function as professionally and rationally as possible.

Perhaps good teaching cannot be defined in a set of competencies or rational behaviors. Perhaps good teaching cannot be explained in a linear fashion. Perhaps good teaching is complex, obscure, and undefinable.

Educational reform movements have included calls for professional accountability. Again, consistent with the patriarchal assumption that males are inherently given the right to control females, a system of regulation has been created over a group of mostly females by those who are predominantly male (e.g., legislators, education administrators, university professors). Teachers are observed, and tested, and their performance is tied to pupil achievement. In a system in which our predetermined outcomes are questionable at best and in which we have never created direct links between teaching and learning, we place teachers under surveillance in which they must display a narrow range of limited behaviors. Otherwise, continued teaching is denied.

Agent of the state. The creation of teachers as agents of the state cannot be separated from the view that women are not competent or sophisticated enough to control their own behavior (Apple, 1983). The state, in the form of professional organizations or government regulations and requirements, must therefore dictate teacher goals and behaviors. Without predetermined expectations and methods of governing practice, unsophisticated teachers would not be able to control the learning of children. Teacher identities are constructed as those who respond to local and state authority, coercing children to become whatever the state has deemed appropriate. Both identities are created by and for the state.

Good daughter. Familiarity with and adherence to predetermined knowledge bases (e.g., child development, appropriate practices) places teachers in the final identity position. With the acquisition and application of dominant views of knowledge, we as females play our essential roles as good daughters. We have learned well the discourses of Rousseau, Freud, Piaget and others who would impose their rational truth on everyone. We serve in our reproductive capacity in the perpetuation of their dominant ideologies. As good daughters, we yield to the control of the patriarchy, whether it is imposed through child development theories, in technical teacher education, or in the doctrine of organizations such as the National Association for the Education of Young Children. Daughters who survive within a patriarchy are not to critique, not to challenge, not to resist. They are to obey.

Discipline and Regulation: The Desire to Judge Oneself

Perhaps the most important issue is the way in which professionalism constructs within teachers and children the desire to be normal and to judge themselves and others as abnormal if particular standards are not met. As discussed in Chapter 4, Foucault (1978) has explained how particular forms of discourse produce desire within human beings, the desire to be useful and productive, the desire to be a contributing part of the community, and the desire to be needed and to help others. The discourse of professionalism constructs these altruistic desires with the expectation that if one follows the standards the desires will be fulfilled. Teachers and children construct themselves based upon the "truth" perpetuated by the discourse, becoming docile bodies managed by outside powers and judging their own worth by the standards of those forces.

Discipline and Desire

Grounded in the discourse of professionalism, schools, medicine, mass media, and most recently professional organizations have constructed concepts of "normality" that internally discipline the self–perceptions of teachers. Women (as the majority of teachers) have learned to judge themselves based on the narrow focus of professional language. Two example agents in the construction of normality regarding early childhood education are the National Association for the Education of Young Children (NAEYC) and the National Board for Professional Teaching Standards (NBPTS). In addition to the doctrine of "developmentally appropriate practice," NAEYC focuses on standards for teacher training programs in early childhood education that are grounded in technique and skills construction. Standards are based on the discourses of child development and learning, curriculum development and implementation, family and community relationships, assessment and evaluation, and professionalism (NAEYC, 1996). First, the construction of the standards is a patriarchal act in which the message is "We as experts rationally know what is best for younger human beings and are the mediators between that knowledge and classroom practice." An example guideline is the following: "Use knowledge of how children develop and learn to provide opportunities that support the physical, social, emotional, language, cognitive, and aesthetic development of all young children from birth through age 8" (NAEYC, p. 14). Those who are "normal" and want the best for others accept the guidelines. Those who do not believe that we can determine a "truth" like child development, or teachers whose cultural or socioeconomic experiences do not lead to the belief in individualized, domain–specific human change are considered radical, uninformed, or not really wanting the best for others.

This disciplinary power abounds in responses to notions that do not fit the dominant ideology. The following are rejected as unenlightened, uncaring, or ignorant:

> *There is no particular way that a two-year-old will act. In some cultures s/he may be skillfully cutting fruit or reproducing communication dances. In others, s/he may be assisting in caring for babies. In still others, s/he may be exerting independence by saying "no."*
> *Everyone is part of our family and must care for other family members. There are no ways that family members of certain ages are expected to perform.*
> *In our society, we expect three– and four–year–olds to read and learn multiple languages. They do this and remain happy and healthy people.*
> *We believe that mind and body are one. We do not separate them as in the United States.*
> *My children want to examine injustice in society. They notice it every day on the TV, at our day care center, and on the streets.*

Good teachers are not to accept such perspectives. Further, teachers are to enlighten parents concerning more educated views. Beliefs that we do not and will never understand how people learn, and that perhaps development and learning are not the types of educational questions that we wish to pursue, are not accepted. Teachers who choose not to advocate for child development are placed in the margins.

The discourse constructs teachers as either successes or failures, responsible for knowing and using the truth in the right way. The following is an example of NBPTS standards: Teachers use their knowledge of child development and their relationships with children and families to understand children as individuals and to plan in response to their unique needs and potentials (NAEYC, 1996). Early in this book, we discussed the problems with child development assumptions, the discourse of the individual, and the ways in which adults have disempowered children by constructing them as needy. In a world in which we want to hear the voices of children without limiting them to our developmentally oriented constructions or our modernist adult/child dichotomies, this standard makes no sense. The standard limits children and their families to benevolent observations and judgment (by experts) and places teachers in a no–win situation. Teachers learn to judge themselves based on "truths" that do not apply to everyone and on the unachievable expectation that they will be successful if professional truths are followed.

Professionalism constructs normality as apolitical because professional truths are considered independent of agendas or values. For example, white middle–class educators continue to display this internalized discipline in their refusal to recognize exploratory play, learning centers, and other forms of child–centeredness as the reproduction of educated, middle–class values. Even the most culturally responsive teacher usually espouses play and exploration as a "better" environment for learning for everyone. "After all, other environments are stressful, require too much of the child, or take away childhood." This view of self as politically neutral results in greater acceptance of the disciplinary power of professionalism without possibility of critical examination. As a group, we only want the best for children. This is not a value that should be questioned.

The discourse of professionalism has so disciplined the desire to "teach well" that educators have accepted professional truth as the standard for judging themselves and others.

There are good teachers and bad teachers. Those who are bad do not follow the professional truths and guidelines.

Educational problems are located in the teachers themselves, in the behaviors of individual bodies (Foucault, 1978). Through the discourse of professionalism, teachers have accepted the blame for all of societies ills, and have reproduced education as patriarchy and control.

Regulation and Desire
The language and actions of professionalism construct regulatory powers within children in which they learn to expect adult control, yield to adult superiority, and accept adult competency. They learn to view themselves as not yet able, as needing the guidance of those who are capable. Children are regulated to desire the help and superiority of those who are older. This language of regulation is adult oriented. The teacher will "select, evaluate, and interpret," "observe, record, and assess" (NAEYC, p. 19), "facilitate positive dispositions" (p. 75), "foster physical health" (p. 72), "use a variety of methods and materials" (p. 66), "work

with and through parents" (p. 66), "create and modify environments" (p. 17), and "focus on children's needs and interests" (p. 17). Children are placed in a position in which they construct themselves as having little or no control. The adult will reveal what is normal, what is expected. Only those who are older possess the power to determine the what and how of the world. Professional discourse and actions construct within children the desire to be helped, to be told who they are, and to be controlled. We teach them how to control their bodies, when to speak and what to say, how to feel and what to think. Only through adults can one become useful, productive and empowered.

Professionalism excludes children from the world of those who are older. In a recent symposium with other early childhood educators, one individual asked, "What do I tell a teacher who believes in using learning centers and child–centered methods but whose parents are pressuring her to use worksheets?" Another educator responded, "You must use both, so that both sides are happy." The questioner was not pleased with the response and furthered the dialogue, asking how the teacher could teach the parents what she knew. Finally, after much discussion, one individual commented, "Should we change the questions that we ask? All of our discussion has been about teachers and parents. We don't even know how to bring children into the dialogue." I would further add that we have taught them to stay away from our "adult" conversations, to expect to be excluded. Exclusion is natural, reasonable, the standard for life.

Professional discourse silences children as it is used to create a "pretend" world for them, a world that has nothing to do with their real lives. As ahistorical, asexual, and asocial views of development and learning are imposed on young human beings (whether by worksheets or learning centers), they are told to be silent. Scientific explanations of them are what counts. The environments that we construct for them should mediate their speech. Children are not yet important enough (stated as mature, competent, advanced cognitively, experienced) to be heard on their own. Adults who understand their lives will speak for them.

Our professional discourse regulates children, constructing the expectation and perhaps desire to be defined by others. They learn to expect to be both excluded and silenced. We have not heard their voices; and we will not as long as they must live within our professional constructions that exert power over them. Our professional discourses legitimize childhood, reducing children to the absolute Other. Embedded in these discourses, we accept and inscribe within children the notion that they are essentially, biologically, and socially different. Because adults are the biggest, strongest, and most rational, we insist that we are naturally superior to children and designed as the political citizens who would control their lives. The adult function is to explain, order, and control the world for children, whether through language experience, phonics, play environments, or worksheets. Although adults and children are human beings, adults function in ways that transcend childhood worlds; we believe that we can both understand these worlds and go beyond them. Children simply function as natural beings with basic needs that adults can fulfill. Adults are viewed as inherently given the right to control children and are the mediators between them and the world. Within our professional discourses, we conclude the work that ultimately and decisively delivers our children "over to the language, rules, and relations of the patriarchy" (Grumet, 1988, p. 56). Their identities are positioned; their self–concepts formed; they have learned to judge and regulate their own normality within sexist, racist, classed societies. They have learned to reason that some are born to rule and others to be ruled.

Challenges to Professionalism

The professionalization of teaching, including early childhood education, has resulted in the perpetuation of patriarchy. However well intended the agenda, the discourses and actions of professionalism have generated disciplinary and regulatory powers over teachers and children.

(1)   Female work has been legitimized as appropriately resulting in lower pay, less autonomy, and increased control. After all, as an inferior group, as those who will be "taken care of" and ruled, females do not require the resources or opportunities that should be given to males.

(2)   Education was constructed as "women's work" because domesticity, self–sacrifice, and submissiveness are to be expected from women. Females were and are constructed as those ideally suited to deliver children to the control and order established by the male world.

(3)   Although serving as a double–edged sword, professionalism in capitalist societies fosters the patriarchal assumptions that one group (the experts, or those who are higher on the professional hierarchy) is superior to another and legitimizes the establishment of order and control by the superior group. Professionalism actually perpetuates the status quo and generates power for a particular group.

(4)   Females, as the group who were taken up by teaching, have been placed at the bottom of the professional ladder and subjected to standardized hiring measures, universalized curriculum policies, and state evaluations. Professionalism has placed women under rigid psychological and technical standards by which we are expected to conform. Those women who exhibit resistance or disagreement are judged as unprofessional.

(5)   As teachers, women's identities are constructed as the good mother (who naturally bonds to children), the gendered worker (who without complaint intensely and continuously works in a deskilled context, placed under the surveillance of those who are superior), the agent of the state (who as an unsophisticated being, yields to the wishes of the state), and the good daughter (who reproduces the patriarchy).

(6)   The discourse of professionalism has constructed concepts of normality that internally discipline the self–perceptions of teachers. They learn to judge themselves based on professional "truths" that locate success or failure within their individual abilities to "teach well." Teaching is constructed as apolitical and locates educational problems within teachers and children, rather than within societal conditions or political power structures.

(7)   The language and actions of professionalism construct regulatory powers within children in which they learn to expect adult control, yield to adult authority, and to judge their own normality within a sexist, racist, classed, and age biased context. Some even learn to desire being ruled by adults or more powerful others.

Our pursuit of professionalism as a way of gaining respect and empowering the field may actually result in a false empowerment. In our attempts to improve the lives of younger human beings, we may actually perpetuate power over them and ourselves. We may even generate the desire and expectation to be told what to do and how to do it. We may create the wish to be regulated, to need to judge ourselves and to make judgements through standards created by others.

Chapter VIII

Reconceptualizing Early Education
as the
Struggle for Social Justice

One could argue that it is politically irresponsible to radically question existing
theoretical political options without taking any responsibility for the impact that
such critique will have and without offering any alternative.

Sawicki, 1991, p. 99

I began this endeavor with the recognition that a critique of the field
that challenged everything that we hold sacred would not be popular.
Questioning the existence of childhood and the truth of child development,
interrogating the methods that we have used with children or presented to
other adults as appropriate, and investigating the hidden assumptions and
agendas in our quest to be professional are not easy. In the language of
enlightenment dualisms, the challenges are not simply objective and
professional, they are personal. Most of us have, in one form or another,
dedicated our lives to protecting and educating younger human beings.
Advocacy for children has been our goal. The possibility that the work of
the field, that our work, may not benefit those who are younger is
threatening and insulting.

Debasing the work of other early childhood educators is not the purpose
of this deconstruction. As some readers may know, I have been very
involved in the discourse of child development, Piagetian constructivism,
and child–centeredness. In the United States and Europe, our lives have
been and are embedded in a political, social, and historical context in which
we have constructed regulatory desires around notions of universal truth,
progress, and hierarchy. These beliefs and desires are part of our culture
and as human constructions (however we might interpret their patriarchal
origins) deserve some form of respect. But, when these constructions are
imposed on all human beings, power relations are produced that foster
injustice, oppression, and regulation. This deconstruction of early
childhood education was conducted to unveil the ways in which our
particular cultural desires, constructions, and beliefs are biased, how our
regimes of truth have been perpetuated, and who has been privileged or
oppressed by dominant perspectives in the field. Diverse analyses can and

will unmask multiple perspectives. This deconstructive project interrupts our official early childhood discourse, revealing silences that we have not considered.

(1)   The creation of the concept of childhood is grounded in enlightenment/modernist cultural bias that places limitations on younger human beings, constructs privilege and power for those who are older, and lessens the connections that we make with children and each other. Science has constructed childhood as the perfect specimen for the scientific gaze, supporting the status quo and perpetuating the colonialist power perspective that legitimizes the notion that one group should have power over another (and can constantly place them under surveillance). The construction of childhood actually reifies those who are younger into simple predetermined entities who are to be regulated, denying their human complexities and ambiguities, and their right to be heard and respected as equal human beings.

(2)   Child development is a discourse that has been constructed within a particular social, political, cultural, and historical context by one group of people with power over other groups. Used to legitimize the surveillance, measurement, control, and categorization of a group of people as normal or deviant, the discourse is linear and deterministic. Child development is an imperialist notion that has fostered dominant power ideologies and produced justification for categorizing children and diverse cultures as backward and as needing help from those who are more "advanced."

(3)   Arising from fear of poor populations and the misogynic need to regulate women, the belief in early experience as the determiner of later life oversimplifies the lives of younger human beings and privileges adults as more sophisticated and intelligent. The belief is ethnocentric, at best, fostering a belief not only in childhood but in one form of childhood. The discourse of early experience locates societal problems either in the individual, the mother, or the family, denying historical, political, or social power relationships.

(4)   In the institutionalization of programs for young children and the
        determination of curricular goals and content, early childhood
        education has played a role in the construction of a two tiered–
        system and in the continued segregation of diverse groups of
        people (e.g., the poor, culturally different, those with diverse
        world views), perpetuating societal beliefs that particular groups
        are inferior to others. Educational truths have been constructed
        and accepted as universal without critique or recognition of the
        political and power context from which they have emerged.

(5)   Within the construction of child–centered pedagogy and play–
        based instruction, a particular group of adults reproduces the
        cultural capital of their own group, legitimizes the power of
        covert control, and creates authority for the surveillance and
        judgment of children. Those who accept child development as
        universal truth, masculine images as superior, and communication
        as a predetermined, "sensitive" process, are privileged. Multiple
        value structures, knowledges, and views of the world are denied.

(6)   The professionalization of teaching has generated disciplinary and
        regulatory powers over women and children through the
        construction of normalized identities and the desire to comply
        with the patriarchal system. Women are expected to accept
        gendered work and to respond to failures as individual
        responsibility, denying the power context or the political nature
        of education. Children are expected to yield to adult authority and
        control, denying their own voice and agency as human beings.

In our constructions of the field, we have not heard the voices of
younger human beings. Forcing them to live within constructions of
"child," "development," and "professional practice," we have denied their
very existence as people living their every days lives. We have created
them as the "Other" who must be spoken for (because they are immature,
incompetent, needy, and lacking) and excluded (because they are innocent,
savage, and require protection). I join with those who have proposed
reconceptualization of our field (Bloch, 1992; Kessler, 1991; Silin, 1995),
suggesting a reconsideration and a reimagining. Reconceptualization would
require concentrated critique, directly confronting the hidden political and

moral agendas that underlie even the best of intentions. The constructions that have dominated the field would be actively challenged. Although refusing to dismiss its power to reveal the beliefs and values of particular groups (Walkerdine, 1984), we might agree to eliminate developmental psychology as a dominant discourse. We could even decide that younger human beings would be better served if not positioned as children, as a group that is "lower" (in multiple ways) than adults. Reconceptualization could result in a field that looks and feels entirely different than the way we know it today, in a field in which the creation of groups of human beings as the Other is actively and vigorously avoided.

Reconceptualization would require new images, potentially images and actions that are controversial, that are disturbingly revolutionary. Within reconceptualization, we would examine our personal and professional values, analyzing the disciplinary and regulatory powers that have produced desires within us and within the field. We would create and confront new educational questions, recognizing that ambiguity and multidirectionality will be part of our everyday lives with other human beings. Reconceptualization would serve as the foundation for continued recognition that whenever we construct other human beings and impose our constructions on them, we not only create the Other but we limit the possibilities that we as educators share with them.

A Reconceptualist Possibility

In 1978, William Pinar explained reconceptualization as beginning with critique, analysis that does not reify existing situations but transforms them (Pinar, 1994). Apple (1975) illustrated this kind of analysis in his critique of the ways in which schools deal with conflict by indoctrinating children into intellectual, political, and cultural passivity, a form of hidden educational curriculum. Recently, in early childhood education, Robin Leavitt (1994) has examined power relations between children and their caregivers focusing on the ways in which child resistance is undermined. Chelsea Bailey, at the University of Wisconsin, is currently exploring the ways in which early childhood education constructs the regulation of children's bodies and the ways in which societal fear of the body is manifest in curriculum. This type of work can transform the conceptualization of curriculum. Reconceptualization is multidirectional and multidimensional, creating new insights grounded in our own work and our own words. Reconceptualization is never finished; it is not a doctrine or an end point, but constant critique from which new constructions emerge.

Agreeing with Pinar's notion of reconceptualization, I do not believe that there is any one way, or one direction, in which we reconceptualize our field. Further, our reconceptualizations will most likely never be entirely separated from the historical, cultural, and political context in which we find ourselves. We are embedded within modernity; the notion of reconceptualization itself is potentially a reaction to modernity. As we reconceptualize, we can function with the recognition that we are contextually grounded and are not discovering universal truths that should be imposed on all human beings. There may always be regimes of truth; our challenge is to recognize the potential danger of our ideas even when they are not presented as truth. Reconceptualizations of the field require new inventions and new languages, constructions that come out of our work as educationists rather than dominant disciplines or capitalist fads. There may be modern constructions that we wish to hold on to, but reconceptualization necessitates continued critique of those constructions, critique that would lead to transformation. Within reconceptualization, we admit to our humanness, that we are value–laden, biased beings whose perspectives and beliefs are often imposed on others without their consent. Reconceptualization is based on our values, but those values and the actions tied to them are continually critiqued, unceasingly analyzed for the power that is generated, the transformations that occur, and the influence that is wielded over fellow human beings.

In a world in which equity (one of the values that I would choose to connect to reconceptualization) is of great importance, reconceptualization would involve sharing our beliefs and biases openly, respecting and valuing multiple realities and possibilities, and constructing a collective vision for action. This vision would be continually critiqued and revised. This type of reconceptualization requires a collective dialogue in which we openly share our values, our aspirations, and our visions for a new beginning. Early childhood educators like Silin (1995), Bloch (1992), and Kessler (1991) have begun this dialogue. The following is my attempt to further the discussion, admitting that the reconceptualization is not a truth, but a possibility for critique that is embedded within my own human beliefs.

I would choose three themes, or more appropriately values, that I would like to see serve as the foundation for dialogue in reconceptualization of the field. The themes are: (1) social justice and equity as the right of younger human beings; (2) education as hearing and responding to the voices of younger human beings in their everyday lives; and (3) professionalism as the development of critical dispositions in the struggle for social justice. These themes are not independent of the context of which I am a part; social justice is a modern notion. Further, the ideas may appear somewhat reactionary, contributing to our dualist forms of thought. However, the themes, or value constructs, could not be viewed as goals that we will achieve in some form of enlightenment/modernist progress toward a predetermined improved end point. Instead, the themes would provide the value base from which we critique and conceptualize; at the same time, the value themes themselves would be under continual examination.

Social Justice as a Human Right

We have constructed the field of early childhood education based on the notion of "child" as psychologically and physically distinct from other human beings. This construct has separated us, denying our human connections. Living within this construct, those who are younger have been controlled, oppressed, labeled, and limited. Their voices have been silenced under the weight of "adult" psychological, educational, and policy constructions of and for them. They must wait to be competent, knowledgeable, and empowered until they reach the privileged position of the adult. Younger human beings are poor, hungry, familiar with violence, and subject to institutionalized assaults on their families, cultures, and values. We send some of them to schools that are dirty, rat infested, and have very few materials while others have all the resources and every opportunity that anyone can imagine. We claim that some have parents who are loving, competent, and intelligent, while we propose that others are in families that do not care, have little judgment, and are damaging. With the exception of those who are white and privileged, our construction of "child" has not improved the lives of younger human beings. Further, even those "children" from privileged groups are placed in the margins of society as inexperienced, immature, innocent, and needing protection from the real world. Our construction of "child" silences a group of human beings, removing all possibility for social justice for them. I recommend that we position "childhood" in the political and historical context from which it emerged, rejecting it as the foundation for our actions.

Rather, social justice and equity as human rights for those who are younger could become the foundation for reconceptualization of the field. Our constructions of social justice would require continual critique but would always focus on broadening possibilities, embracing the struggle for liberation, avoiding constructions of the Other, and aiming for just and caring communities (Giroux & Simon, 1989). Further, the power relations that have been constructed within the patriarchal value structure that is the institution of education would be acknowledged and continually evaluated. New questions would be asked:

How do we construct equitable partnerships with each other in which everyone's voice is actually heard?
What are the underlying messages in our beliefs, goals, and actions?
Who is damaged? Who is silenced?
Are we challenging forms of oppression? Who is exercising power? What does this power produce?
Do we function as if our own questions represent regimes of truth?

We would become partners with younger human beings, their families, and their communities in establishing goals for action that included recognition, decolonization, the struggle for justice, and the creation of caring communities in which all are justly perceived. Social justice could not be constructed without an "ethic of care" (Noddings, 1992), a form of regard in which each person (including the body) is respected and viewed as integral to the human connection (Martin, 1986). We would strive to eliminate dualisms that separate us into multiple identities in one body or that prejudice us against each other as separate human bodies. Knowledge and interpersonal relationships would always be integrated because being with other human beings would function as a form of caring (Silin, 1995). Social justice demands active involvement in and with the multiple worlds of the child, expanding from the narrow confines of preschools, elementary schools, and child care programs. For example, when younger human beings (or any human beings) live in inequitable physical environments in which those in power have allowed sewage back-up or other toxic conditions (Kozol, 1991), workers in a field whose foundation is social justice would not be silent, would fight for revolution. Living within an "ethic of care," we would not be ignorant of the lives and worlds of others. We could not ignore or disqualify their lives as simply unfortunate or deserving sympathy.

Can we practice social justice for younger human beings and still place them in schools or institutionalized child care? Most forms of schooling (if not all) have been conceptually constructed as mechanisms of control, as ways to protect, discipline, and regulate the learning of others. Social justice has not really even been a point of discussion regarding those who are not considered adults. The physical placement of their human bodies into controlled environments for much of their lives is an issue that would certainly require consideration as a point of social justice. In the United States, the issue would generate as much debate as abortion or sexual orientation. As we choose our struggles, we could at least begin by addressing social justice within and around institutionalized settings:

How do we eliminate a two–tiered system?
Does the curriculum respect the multiple knowledges and life experiences of younger human beings from diverse backgrounds?
How does our current practice perpetuate a classed structure in society?
Is the message provided by education to each human being equitable regarding his or her background, beliefs, and life experiences?
Does the educational/care system treat everyone fairly and with respect?
Are there those whose life experiences create privilege for them within the school contexts that we have created? Is this socially just?

The belief that social justice can be achieved for everyone, not only perpetuates the notions of progress and predetermined outcomes, but overly simplifies and reifies the lives of human beings. Our lives are multidirectional, ambiguous, and indeterminate. We appear caught up in webs of power, in fields of conflict and struggle that hold within them possibilities for both liberation and control (Foucault, 1983; Sawicki, 1991). We seem to construct discourses that are used to both regulate and liberate. As complex human beings, we know that our quest for social justice will most likely always be a struggle, a continuous encounter with multiple agendas, diverse values, and contradictory views of how we can treat and respect each other. Social justice could not be the final outcome of a goal. Rather, social justice would be the value that permeates our bodies, that runs through every decision that we make, the value that saturates the field.

Education as Hearing and Responding

As educators, we have continually made decisions for others, constructing the languages with which they should speak, the materials that they should use, and the ways of thinking that should control their bodies. Most of us create classrooms (and teach others to create classrooms) that set the parameters for the speech, behavior, and activity of others. Whether using learning centers, worksheets, group activities, or independent experiences, all establish disciplinary and regulatory powers over others. Further, most are grounded in psychological constructions of learning and perpetuate some form of the psychologized child. The most recent examples in early childhood education include the focus on Piagetian constructivist programs and the creation and marketing of developmentally appropriate practice. Within a Piagetian perspective, only the voices of those who would conform to modernist logic can be heard. The voices of those who would challenge the use or universality of that logic, whether younger or older, are disqualified, ignored, or placed in the margin as developmentally immature, culturally deficient, lacking in understanding, or radical. The language of developmentally appropriate practice places everyone in the position of speaking with a white, middle-class enlightenment voice, whether that voice is understood or supported. Again, models of learning, management and intervention, and psychologized, even developmental, views of education have arisen from particular historical and political contexts and have played a dominant role in the creation of hegemony and oppression. With the exception of those who have been strong enough to resist, the voices of younger human beings have not been heard within our constructions of education. Further, the voices and the constructions of those who are older have dominated their lives. Younger human beings have been silenced. I would again recommend that we recognize the historical and political embeddedness of our constructions of education and position those constructions in ways that they do not silence diverse groups of human beings.

I would further challenge early childhood educators to reconceptualize the field as one in which younger human beings not only create their own voices, but that we in our research and practice make every attempt to actually hear what is being said (Delpit, 1993). First, to hear younger human beings, we must challenge our conceptions of them as the Other, those who are heard only within the constructions that we have created of them, or those who cannot speak for themselves. Perhaps two-year-olds appear to exert independence by saying "No" because this is the construction of them that we have created. Those younger human beings who care for family members may never reveal this voice because it does not fit with our perceptions of them as needing protection themselves. All four-year-olds do not ask continuous "Why" questions; perhaps those who do have simply yielded to the dominant rules that we create for them. To hear those who have most often been ignored, silenced, and even perceived as having no voice, we must accept them as real, legitimate human beings. We must accept that they can speak for themselves and search for ways that we can learn to listen.

Early childhood educators can receptualize the field as active involvement in the dismantling of stereotypes in which the voices of young human beings are categorized as unfit, ineligible, or disqualified. These classifications are grounded in the adult privilege that is created in the construction of the concept of immaturity and in patriarchal notions of cognition and language acquisition. Further, diverse forms of voice are ignored. Apple (1993) reminds us that there has always been resistance, voices who have refused to go unheard. However, we have tended to romanticize these voices, placing them in the margins of normality, constructing the belief that resistant voices either revealed special gifts or proved deviance. Further, voices of resistance have not often been successful. As human beings and as early childhood educators, we have not heard the voices around us, much less responded to their messages.

Additionally, we have not heard or respected the multiple voices influencing younger human beings in their worlds outside of our "control," unless we perceive those voices as either supporting or preventing the attainment of our goals. Delpit (1986) illustrates the ways in which liberal educators foster silence by advocating the notion that discovery–oriented, whole–language based experiences give minority children voice. She points out, however, that when minority teachers and parents disagree and provide their own understanding of minority survival, those same liberal educators will not listen. Are we really open to diverse voices if we only listen when the language is consistent with what we want to hear? The diverse everyday lives of young human beings, and the voices of their families and communities in those everyday lives, must be accepted as legitimate, multidimensional, and worthy of being heard.

To hear and respond to the voices of younger human beings, we must admit that we have not listened and that we often do not know how to hear.

Further, there are no predetermined methods for us to discover that would enable us to hear everyone. Beginnings can be found in the use of "radical" methods such as body knowing (Dewey, 1899/1959), involvement in the arts (Coe, 1984), and phenomenological methods (Weber, 1984). However, our major hope is to jointly participate with younger human beings in the real world, in the world outside of the controlled classrooms that we have created for them. This participation in the real world may be dangerous. Younger human beings should have the right to refuse our participation, to resist any form of colonization that our involvement in their lives might produce. If they and their families want to explore ways in which we can share in each other's lives, we may not always be comfortable. The voices may not be consistent with our middle–class, educated dialogues. Contexts, identities, and positions of power may shift, requiring us to live with the ambiguity, uncertainty, and disturbance that comes with hearing multiple voices. We could conceptualize a field in which education is viewed as hearing and responding to the voices of younger members of society, in which we continually search for ways to connect our human lives to each other.

Professionalism as the Pursuit of Social Justice

As early childhood educators, we have constructed a field and supported a profession that is grounded in the best of intentions. We have advocated for children more than any other group. Even the current push for Piagetian methods and developmentally appropriate practice is a form of advocacy by those who do not want younger human beings to be chained to a desk and forced to do worksheets for hours (an experience that could be negative for any of us, at any age). We must, however, face the possibility that whatever our intentions, we have constructed the lives of others in our middle–class, hierarchical image. Our actions have been grounded in psychologically biased knowledge that has supported the patriarchal condition that we might hope to challenge. As professionals, we have legitimized the notion that males rule females and adults rule children. As a final challenge, I would propose that professionalism in the field of early childhood education become the development of critical dispositions in the struggle for social justice and care.

This new professionalism would require that we reject the view of education and educators as apolitical, accepting the power–oriented, political nature of schooling. We would explore the possibility that political neutrality actually supports the dominant ideology, perpetuating the status quo (Kincheloe, 1993). Professionalism would no longer be a way to illustrate for others that we are intelligent and worthy, but a call to action in ways that foster social justice. Professionalism would no longer be the safe path that assures patriarchal forms of respect for women, but a dangerous journey in the struggle for just and caring communities.

The construction of critical dispositions would require that we learn to interrogate the social, cultural, linguistic, and power context in which our belief structures and educational practices have been constructed. New questions would be asked:

> *What is meant by social justice for younger human beings?*
> *What are critical dispositions and how do we develop them?*
> *How do our daily behaviors contribute to oppression or privilege?*
> *What are the underlying messages of this social policy? Who actually benefits from the perspective?*
> *Are we hearing and responding to the diverse voices of younger human beings without silencing those who are older?*
> *How has society objectified children? In what ways are they objectified by institutionalized education and care?*
> *How do we reconceptualize our daily experiences with younger human beings in ways that contribute to social justice?*
> *Are we collaborating with those who are younger in our understanding of social justice?*
> *How does a critical disposition influence each of us in our lives away from early childhood education?*
> *How can we expand our boundaries to include those who have been marginalized, to eliminate their exclusion?*
> *How can human connections be created that contribute to social justice?*
> *How do we avoid constructing regimes of truth, even as related to social justice.*

Ultimately we must construct our own views of social justice, our own ways of hearing other human beings, and our own critical dispositions. The work of scholars such as Foucault (1965, 1970, 1977, 1978, 1980) can, however, help us begin. His work reveals the sites of authority through which we are constituted, the power relationships within our everyday discourse, our cultural representations, and our hidden histories. The work of feminists (Jipson, 1992; Noddings, 1992; Walkerdine, 1990), critical theorists (Giroux & McLaren, 1989;   Kincheloe, 1993;), and queer theorists (Cruikshank, 1982; Garber, 1994) can provide further guidance.

Finally, a professionalism grounded in social justice would welcome controversy and conflict in the name of justice for younger human beings. Actions fostering social justice would be understood as potentially unpopular and threatening to the dominant perspective. The profession would accept challenge, critique, reconceptualization, and even revolution if necessary in the pursuit of just and equitable treatment for all human beings. Those in the profession would not be those who comply with truth constructed by those in power, but partners with younger human beings in the human struggle.

Revolutionary Images

If early childhood education were reconceptualized as the pursuit of social justice for younger human beings, new images could emerge as the framework for action. These images could include (but would not be limited to) a struggle to learn how to respect others, the recognition of multiple realities, the belief in the inhumanity of creating others as objects, the practice of radical democracy, and the willingness to take revolutionary action. Education would become a radical journey in which we would all struggle to learn about ourselves and each other, struggling with the recognition that our histories, our beliefs, our facts, even our lives are ever changing, subjective, and indeterminate. We would understand that our images for the construction of social justice must be rebellious, must overthrow the status quo, must challenge sites of power.

Human respect. Perceived differently by different cultural groups, respect for all human beings is not simple or easily definable. However, within the context of social justice and care, respect would require appreciation of the value of all other beings, acceptance of multiple ways of thinking and being in the world, and a willingness to fight for an equitable and just community for everyone. The separation of child and adult, as currently conceptualized, would be recognized as dehumanizing to younger human beings, as creating a situation in which those who are younger are not even accepted as participants in the struggle for social justice. Practicing respect for all others would be a continuous struggle to learn how to see, hear, and appreciate everyone, including those who have been constructed as not yet competent, as immature, as poor, as different than the accepted self.

Multiple realities. Without the acceptance of multiple human realities as legitimate and of value, those who believe that they possess the truth for everyone will always control the lives of others. Reductionist perspectives have silenced many of us, including those who are younger. To actually share in the lives of others, to hear and respond to their voices, multiple knowledges, ways of knowing, and being in the world must be affirmed (Silin, 1995). Multiple human realities will require that we become comfortable with uncertainty, that we accept ambiguity. We will not recognize or understand all realities, but must construct a view of the world in which we strive to accept, understand, and value diverse constructions and perspectives of the world.

Subjectivity/Agency. Generally, education has constructed other human beings as those to be controlled, whether as teachers or as children. Creating others as objects to be observed, measured, judged, or otherwise manipulated is an act of injustice. The conceptualization of education as the pursuit of social justice would require that all human beings be appreciated as the subjects and agents of their own lives. This would not and should not lead to holding individuals responsible for societal conditions that are beyond their control, but to the recognition that all, including those who are younger, deserve to be heard and accepted as initiators of action and forces in the world.

Radical democracy. The practice of radical democracy goes beyond any simplistic acceptance of equal representation for all, one-person-one-vote, or the privileging of capitalist democratic competition. Radical democracy would always strive to critique itself and would embrace difference and dialogue as well as the struggle for equity and justice. All members of society, especially those who are younger, would be both encouraged and supported in claiming their own cultures, histories, and voices (Macedo, 1994). We would not accept the notion that human actions are neutral, but recognize that the struggle for power between diverse discourses is always political. Radical democratic practices would be messy, could not be predetermined, but would always involve the analysis of power and the ways in which power was generated over people.

Revolutionary action. In the pursuit of social justice, we would expect to take actions that would not always be popular, that would draw criticism as the status quo and those in power were challenged. We would all become revolutionaries in the struggle for democracy, for equitable and caring relations. Those who are younger would be accepted as equal partners in our struggle. As early childhood educators, we would collaborate with them, their families, and their communities to construct education that fostered social justice both within the walls of schools and outside. We would become revolutionaries who construct critical actions, and continuously analyze those actions as to their effect on ourselves and others. Social justice and care would be the values that would be the foundation for our revolt.

Fostering Reconceptualization

In proposing reconceptualization, I have been asked "How do we tell our preservice teachers to work with children? How do they construct their classrooms?" I believe that our modernist discourses have led us to these questions and allowed us to eliminate from our conceptualizations other, more ambiguous possibilities. Rather then "What do I do on Monday?" we might ask questions concerning the construction of new discourses, the role of power relationships in our reconceptualizations, the elimination of boundaries between resistance, research, and practice, and the examination of policy as applicable to a field that has been transformed. Perhaps our collaborations with younger human beings will lead us and our preservice teachers to new conceptualizations of what to do on Monday. Perhaps there would be no school on Monday; maybe we would work together in the community on specific social justice issues; or perhaps actions would not be predetermined.

The language practices that currently dominate our thoughts represent the discourses of patriarchy. Living within these dominant ways of using language, we would be expected to express concern over "what to do on Monday." Our present forms of discourse represent enlightenment/ modernist thought (as evidenced in the dichotomous ways in which we speak) and patriarchal expressions of power and determinism (as evidenced in the belief that one should know what to do). Walkerdine (1990) argues that we must construct discourses and actions that do not perpetuate modernist or patriarchal thought. As examples, using the words "needy," "helpless," and "protect" regarding a particular group of people constructs the patriarchal expectation that some are superior to others and legitimizes the us of power over them. Continued use of dichotomous language (male/female, adult/child, right/wrong, moral/immoral, mind/body) fosters simplistic notions of the ways that human beings function and marginalizes those who do not fit into any category or are not part of the category of power. Within reconceptualization, we would construct new discourses, languages of social justice and care, languages created by those who are younger, and languages of critique. Our discourses would foster human connections and equity (e.g., solidarity, empathy) rather than patriarchy and separation (e.g., expert/novice, appropriate/inappropriate).

As Skrtic (1995) explains, we are all caught in the multiple webs of power in society. Power is not simply created by evil politicians or power hungry professionals. "Power relations are established within historical fields of conflict and struggle" (Sawicki, 1991, p. 56). No discourse is free of power relations, including reconceptualization and the construction of new forms of language. To foster social justice and to hear the voices of others (even those others who do not agree with social justice), a critical disposition is necessary so that our reconceptualization does not become the new regime of truth.

To return to our concern for how to work with children on Monday, the question represents the research/practice dualism, constructed through modernist rationalization. The research gives us a reasoned logic and the practice tells us what to do. Hearing and responding to the voices of younger human beings not only eliminates this separation as a possibility, but introduces the notion of resistance. We will not hear the voices of others if research is viewed as prophecy (Popkewitz, 1996) or as rescue mission (Viswasnaran, 1994). We will not hear the voices of others if practice is viewed as control, predetermination, and outcome. Reconceptualization would lead us to abolish the boundaries that are constructed between research and practice and to place resistance at the center. Work in early childhood education would become the resistance to dominant forces that inhibit social justice and the caring tasks of hearing the voices of others. This work could be found in classrooms, communities, and even in scholarly research publications.

Until this point, we have not addressed the issue of policy. Determining what happens to others as a result of our reconceptualization(s) is of utmost importance. Policy is perhaps the dominant, yet invisible, issue embedded within the struggle for social justice. To hear and respect the voices of all groups of younger human beings and to avoid the unnecessary discipline or regulation of anyone, social justice must be at the forefront of our thoughts. Further, our reconceptualist ideas could be used by local power brokers who wish to eliminate rights for particular groups, construct their own perspectives as dominant, or place themselves in positions of economic gain. A professionalism that fosters critique from multiple perspectives becomes an absolute necessity.

Final/Beginning Thoughts

To reconceptualize a field in which social justice and hearing the voices of younger human beings are the foundation, we must be willing to expand our possibilities, to go beyond the ways that we have been taught to perceive. My colleagues have disagreed with these radical ideas for early childhood education, calling them "too revolutionary." Some believe that the ideas can cause trouble. I believe that we want to cause trouble, that we need to transform ourselves into revolutionary activists for social justice and care, not simply for younger human beings, but for all of us. Only when we are willing to transform ourselves and our work do we have the possibility of transforming society (Pinar, 1994). "When any of us must endure inequity or injustice, when there are those who are not heard, as human beings we are all diminished" (Cannella, in press).

References

Agger, B. (1991). Critical theory, poststructuralism, postmodernism: Their sociological relevance. In W.R. Scott & J. Blake (Eds.), *Annual review of sociology, Vol. 17* (pp. 105-31). Palo Alto, CA: Annual Reviews, Inc.

Ainsworth, M.D.S. (1967). *Infancy in Uganda: Infant care and the growth of attachment.* Baltimore, MD: Johns Hopkins University Press.

Anderson, C.A. (1966). The modernization of education. In M. Weiner (Ed.), *Modernization: The dynamics of growth* (pp. 68-80). New York: Basic Books.

Anderson, L.F. (1970). *Pestalozzi.* New York: AMS Press.

Apple, M.W. (1975). The hidden curriculum and the nature of conflict. In W. Pinar (Ed.), *Curriculum theorizing : The reconceptualists* (pp. 95-119). Berkeley: McCutchan.

Apple, M.W. (1983). Work, gender, and teaching. *Teachers College Record, 84*(3), 611-628.

Apple, M.W. (1987). Gendered teaching, gendered labor. In T. Popkewitz (Ed.) *Critical studies in teacher education: Its folklore, theory, and practice* (pp. 57-83). New York: Falmer Press.

Apple, M.W. (1993). *Official knowledge: Democratic education in a conservative age.* New York: Routledge.

Apple, M.W. (1996). *Cultural politics and education.* New York: Teachers College Press.

Appleby, J., Hunt, L., & Jacob, M. (1994). *Telling the truth about history.* New York: W.W. Norton.

Aries, P. (1962). *Centuries of childhood—A social history of family life.* New York: Knopf.

Aristotle (1941). *Politica.* In R. McKeon (Ed.) *The basic works of Aristotle.* New York: Random House.

Ausubel, D.P. (1963). *The psychology of meaningful verbal learning.* New York: Grune & Stratton.

Bailey, C. (working paper). *The curriculum of the body: A young child's life in school.* Madison, WI: The University of Wisconsin.

Banks, J. (1993). The canon debate, knowledge construction and multicultural education. *Educational Researcher, 22*(5), 4-14.

Barber, E. (1943). Marriage and the family after the war. *Annals of the American Academy of Political and Social Science, 229.*

Barnard,H. (1890) *Kindergarten and child culture papers: The American journal of education.* Hartford, CT.

Blanchot, M. (1989). *Michel Foucault as I imagine him.* (J. Mehlman, Trans.). New York: Zone Books.

Bleir, R. (1984). *Science and gender: A critique of biology and its theories on women.* New York: Pergamon.

Bloch, E. (1986). *The principle of hope.* Oxford: Basil Blackwell.

Bloch, M.N. (1987). Becoming scientific and professional: An historical perspective on the aims and effects of early education. In T.S. Popkewitz (Ed.), *The formation of school subjects* (pp. 25-62). Basingstoke, England: Falmer.

Bloch, M.N. (1992). Critical perspectives on the historical relationship between child development and early childhood education research. In S. Kessler & B. B. Swadener (Eds.) *Reconceptualizing the early childhood curriculum: Beginning the dialogue* (pp. 3-20). New York: Teachers College Press.

Bloch, M.N. & Adler, S. A. (1994). African children's play and the emergence of the sexual division of labor. In J.L Roopnarine, J.E. Johnson, & F.H. Hooper (Eds.). *Children's play in diverse cultures.* Albany, NY: State University of New York Press.

Block, A.A. (1995). "Its alright, ma (i 'm only bleeding)": Education as the practice of social violence against the child. *TABOO: The Journal of Culture and Education, 1,*121-142.

Bloom, B. (1964). *Stability and change in human characteristics.* New York: Wiley.

Bowlby, J. (1951). *Maternal care and mental health.* Geneva: World Health Organization.

Bowlby, J. (1958). The nature of the child's tie to his mother. *International Journal of PsychoAnalysis, 38*(9), 350-72.

Boyden, J. (1990). Childhood and the policy makers: A comparative perspective on the globalization of childhood. In A. James & A. Prout (Eds.),*Constructing and reconstructing childhood: Contemporary issues in the sociological study of childhood* (pp. 184-215). Basingstoke, Hants: Falmer.

Boyer, E.L. (1993). Ready to learn: A mandate for the nation. *Young Children, 48*(3), 54-57.

Bradley, B.S. (1989). *Visions of infancy.* Oxford: Polity/Blackwell.

Bredekamp, S. (Ed.), (1987). *Developmentally appropriate practice in early childhood programs serving children from birth through age eight.* Washington, DC: National Association for the Education of Young Children.

Broughton, J.M. (1987). An introduction to critical developmental psychology. In J.M. Broughton (Ed.). *Critical theories of psychological development* (pp. 1-30). New York: Plenum Press.

Brown, E., Martinez, P., & Radke-Yarrow. (Fall, 1992). Diversity: Research with diverse populations. *Society for Research in Child Development Newsletter*, pp. 2, 12.

Buck-Morss, S. (1975). Socio-economic bias in Piaget's theory and its implications for cross-cultural studies. *Human Development, 18*, 35-45.

Burman, E. (1994). *Deconstructing developmental psychology.* New York: Routledge.

Bury, J.B. (1932). *The idea of progress: An inquiry into its origin and growth.* New York: Dover Publications, Inc.

Butterfield, L.H., Friedlaender, M., & Kline, M.J. (Eds.), (1975). *The book of Abigail and John: Secected letters of the Adams family.* Cambridge, MA: Harvard University Press.

Cahan, E., Mechling, J., Sutton-Smith, B., & White, S.H. (1993). The elusive historical child: Ways of knowing the child of history and psychology. In G.H. Elder, Jr., J. Model, & R. D. Parke (Eds.), *Children in time and place: Developmental and historical insights* (pp. 192-223). New York: Cambridge University Press.

Caldwell, B. (1984). Growth and development. *Young Children, 39*(6), 53-56.

Cannella, G.S. (in press) Early childhood education: A call for the construction of revolutionary images. In W.F. Pinar (Ed.), *Curriculum: Toward new identities in/for the field.* Garland.

Castel, R. (1994). "Problematization" as a mode of reading history. In J. Goldstein (Ed.), *Foucault and the writing of history* (pp. 237-304). Cambridge, MA: Blackwell.

Cherryholmes, C. (1988). *Power and criticism: Poststructural investigations in education.* New York: Teachers College Press.

Chodorow, N. (1978). *The reproduction of mothering: Psychoanalysis and the sociology of gender.* Berkeley: University of California Press.

Clark, E. (1989). *Young single mothers today: A qualitative study of housing and support needs.* London: National Council for One Parent Families.

Clarke, A.M., & Clarke, A.D.B. (1976). *Early experience: Myth and evidence.* London: Open Books.

Cleverley, J., & Phillips, D.C. (1986). *Visions of childhood: Influential models from Locke to Spock.* New York: Teachers College Press.

Coe, R.N. (1984). *When the grass was taller: Autobiography and the experience of childhood.* New Haven, CT: Yale University Press.

Collins, P.H. (1989). A comparison of two works on black family life. *Signs: Journal of Women in Culture and Society, 14*(4), 875-884.

Comenius, J.A. (1967). *The great diadactic of John Amos Comenius.* (M.W. Keating, Trans. and Ed.). New York: Russell & Russ. (Original work published 1896)

Connolly, K., & Bruner, J. (1974). *The growth of competence.* New York: Academic Press.

Cooke, W. (1944). The differential psychology of American women. *American Journal of Obstetric Gynocology, 57,* 466-70.

Crocker, L.S. (1968-73). *Jean-Jacques Rousseau.* New York: Macmillan.

Cruikshank, M. (Ed.). (1982). *Lesbian studies: Present and future.* New York: Feminist Press.

Dally, A. (1983). *Inventing motherhood: The consequences of an ideal.* New York: Schocken.

Dardess, J. (1991). Childhood in pre-modern China. In J. M. Hawes & N. R. Hiner (Eds.), *Children in historical and comparative perspective* (pp. 71-98). Westport, CT: Greenwood Press.

Darwin, C. (1979) *The illustrated origin of species.* (R. E. Leakey, Abrigded and Introduced.). New York: Hill and Wang. (Original work published 1859)

Darwin, C. (1859). *On the origin of species by means of natural selection.* London: John Murray.

Davis, Jr., O. (1986). ASCD and curriculum development: The later years. In W. van Til (Ed.), *ASCD in restropect: Contributions to the history of the Association for Supervision and Curriculum Development* (pp. 83-93). Alexandria, VA: Association for Supervision and Curriculum Development.

Degler, C. (1980). *At odds: Women and the family in America from the revolution to the present.* London: Oxford University Press.

DeGuimps, R. (1890). *Pestalozzi: His life and work.* New York: D. Appleton and Company.

Delpit, L. (1993). The silenced dialogue: Power and pedagogy in educating other people's children. In L. Weis, & M. Fine (Eds.), *Beyond silenced voices: Class, race, and gender in United States schools* (pp. 119-139). Albany: SUNY Press.

Delpit, L. (1995). *Other people's children: Cultural conflict in the classroom.* New York: The New Press.

deMarrais, K.B., Nelson, P.A. & Baker, J.H. (1994). Meaning in mud: Yup'ik Eskimo girls at play. In J.L. Roopnarine, J.E. Johnson & F. H. Hooper (Eds.). *Children's play in diverse cultures* (pp. 179-209). Albany: State University of New York Press.

deMause, L. (1974). *The history of childhood.* New York: The Psychohistory Press.

Densmore, K. (1987). Professionalism, proletarianization and teacher work. In T. Popkewitz (Ed.), *Critical studies in teacher education: Its folklore, theory, and practice* (pp. 130-160). New York: Falmer Press.

Derrida, J. (1981). *Dissemination*. (B. Johnson, Trans.). Chicago: University of Chicago Press.

DeVries, R., & Zan, B. (1994). *Moral classrooms, moral children: Creating a constructivist atmosphere in early education*. New York: Teachers College Press.

DeVries, R., & Kohlberg, L. (1987/1990). *Constructivist early education: Overview and comparison with other programs*. Washington, DC: National Association for the Education of Young Children.

Dewey, J. (1944). *Democracy and education*. New York: Free Press. (Original work published 1916)

Dewey, J. (1959). The school and society. In M.S. Dworkin (Ed.), *Dewey on education* (pp. 33-90). New York: Teachers College Press. (Original work published 1899).

Dews, P. (1987). *Logics of disintegration: Post-structuralist thought and the claims of critical theory*. London: Verso.

Donzelot, J. (1979). *The policing of families*. New York: Pantheon.

Durkheim, E., & Mauss, M. (1963). *Primitive classification*. Chicago: University of Chicago Press.

Dworetsky, J. (1990). *Introduction to child development*. St. Paul, MN: West.

Edwards, C., Gandini, L., & Forman, G. (1993). *The hundred languages of children: The Reggio Emilia approach to early childhood education*. Norwood, NJ: Ablex.

Egerton, J. (1991). The family way: Labour's policy on the family. *Trouble and Strife, 20,* 3-7.

Ehrenreich, B., & English, D. (1978). *For her own good: 150 years of the "experts" advice to women.* New York: Doubleday.

Erikson, E.H. (1950). *Childhood and society.* New York: W.W. Norton.

Eyer, D.E. (1992). *Mother-infant bonding: A scientific fiction.* New Haven: Yale University Press.

Ferreiro, E., & Teberosky, A. (1979/1982). *Literacy before schooling.* Portsmouth, NH: Heinemann.

Fillmore, L.W. (1991). When learning a second language means losing the first. *Early Childhood Research Quarterly, 6*(3), 323-346.

Foucault, M. (1965) *Madness and civilization: A history of insanity in the age of reason.* New York: Pantheon.

Foucault, M. (1970). *The order of things: An archaeology of the human sciences.* New York: VintageBooks.

Foucault, M. (1972). *The archaeology of knowledge.* (A.M.S. Smith, Trans.). New York: Pantheon.

Foucault, M. (1977). *Discipline and punish: The birth of the prison.* New York: Pantheon.

Foucault, M. (1978). *The history of sexuality: Vol's I –III.* New York: Pantheon.

Foucault, M. (1980). *Power/Knowledge: Selected interviews and other writings 1972-1977.* New York: Pantheon.

Foucault, M. (1983). The subject and power: Afterward to Hubert Dreyfus and Paul Rabinou. *Michel Foucault: Beyond structuralism and hermeneutics* (pp. 208–264). Chicago: University of Chicago Press.

Frank, L.K. (July, 1938). The fundamental needs of the child. *Mental Hygiene, 22,* 353-79.

Freire, P., & Macedo, D. (1987). *Literacy: Reading the word and the world.* Westport, CN: Bergin & Garvey.

French, V. (1991). Children in antiquity. In J.M. Hawes, & N.R. Hiner (Eds.), *Children in historical and comparative perspective* (pp. 13–30). Westport, CT: Greenwood Press.

Freud, S. (1925, 1962). *Three contributions to the theory of sex.* (A.A. Brill, Trans.). New York: Dutton.

Froebel, F. (1887). *The education of man.* (M.W. Hailman, Trans.). New York: D. Appleton and Company.

Fuller, P. (1979). Uncovering childhood. In M. Hoyles (Ed.), *Changing childhood* (pp. 71-108). London: Readers and Writers Cooperative.

Furstenberg, F., Brooks-Gunn, J., & Morgan, S.P. (1987). *Adolescent mothers in later life.* Cambridge: Cambridge University Press.

Garber, L. (Ed.). (1994). *Tilting the tower.* New York: Routledge.

Garcia, E., & McLaughlin, B. (Eds.). (1995). *Meeting the challenge of linguistic and cultural diversity in early childhood education.* New York: Teachers College Press.

Gesell, A., & Ilg, F. L. (1949). *Child development.* New York: Harper & Row.

Gibson, E., & Walk, R.D. (1973). The "visual cliff." In T. Greenough (Ed.). *The nature and nurture of behavior: Developmental psychobiology* (pp. 19-26). San Francisco: Freeman. (Original work in Scientific American, April, 1960)

Gilligan, C. (1982). *In a different voice: Psychological theory and women s development.* Cambridge, MA: Harvard University Press.

Ginsburg, M. (1987). Reproduction, contradiction and conceptions of professionalism: The case of pre-service teachers. In T. Popkewitz (Ed.), *Critical studies in teacher education: Its folklore, theory, and practice* (pp. 86-129). New York: Falmer Press.

Giroux, H.A., & McLaren, P. (Eds.). (1989). *Critical pedagogy, the state, and cultural struggle.* Albany, NY: State University of New York Press.

Giroux, H.A., & Simon, R. (1989). Popular culture and critical pedagogy: Everyday life as a basis for curriculum knowledge. In H.A. Giroux & P. McLaren, P. (Eds.), *Critical pedagogy, the state, and cultural struggle.* (pp. 236-252). Albany: State University of New York Press.

Golding, S. (1992). *Gramsci's democratic theory: Contributions to a post-liberal democracy.* Toronto: University of Toronto Press.

Good, H., & Teller, J. (1969). *A history of western education.* New York: Macmillan.

Goodwin, M.H. (1990). *He said/she said: Talk as social organization among black children.* Bloomington: Indiana University Press.

Gordon, M.M. (1991). Australia and New Zealand. In J.M. Hawes, & N.R. Hiner (Eds.), *Children in historical and comparative perspective* (pp. 97–146). Westport, CT: Greenwood Press.

Gould, S.J. (1981). *The mismeasure of man.* New York: W.W. Norton.

Graue, M.E. (1993). *Ready for what? Constructing meanings of readiness for kindergarten.* Albany, NY: State University of New York Press.

Grimshaw, J. (1986). *Philosophy and feminist thinking.* Minneapolis: University of Minnesota Press.

Grumet, M. R. (1988). *Bitter milk: Women and teaching.* Amherst: University of Massachusetts Press.

Hamilton, D. (1990). *Curriculum history.* Geelong, Victoria, Australia: Deakin University Press.

Hamilton, D. (1989). *Toward a theory of schooling.* London: Falmer.

Haraway, D. (1989). *Primate visions: Gender, race, and nature in the world of modern science.* London: Verso.

Harlow, H. (1973). Love in infant monkeys. In T. Greenough (Ed.), *The nature and nurture of behavior: Developmental psychobiology* (pp. 94–100). San Francisco: Freeman. (Original work published in *Scientific American* in July, 1959)

Harris, A. (1987). The rationalisation of infancy. In J. Broughton (Ed.). *Critical theories of psychological development.* (pp 31-60). New York: Plenum Press.

Heath, S.B. (1983). *Ways with words: Language, life, and work in communities and classrooms.* New York: Cambridge University Press.

Heider, K.G. (1977). From Javanese to Dani: The translation of a game. In P. Stevens (Ed.). *Studies in the anthropology of play* (pp. 72–80). West Point, NY: Leisure Press.

Hendrick, H. (1990). Constructions and reconstructions of British childhood: An interpretive survey, 1800 to present. In A. James & A. Prout (Eds.), *Constructing and reconstructing childhood: Contemporary issues in the sociological study of childhood* (pp. 35-59). Basingstoke, Hants: Falmer.

House of Commons. (1988). Educational provision for the under-fives. *First Report of the Education, Science and Arts Committee,* Vol. 1. London, HMSO.

Howes, E.P. (1923, December). The nursery school. *Woman's Home Companion, 50,* 34.

Hoyles, M. (1979). *Changing Childhood*. London: Writers and Readers Publishing Cooperative.

Hrdy, S.B. (1995, December). Natural-born mothers. *Natural History*, *104*(12), 30-42.

Hume, D. (1982). Section III: Treatise of human nature. In J.B. Wilbur & H.J. Allen (Eds.), *The worlds of Hume and Kant* (pp. 15-20). Buffalo, NY: Prometheus Books.

Hunt, J. (1961). *Intelligence and experience*. New York: Ronald.

Hunt, P. & Frankenberg, R. (1990). It's a small world: Disneyland, the family and the multiple re-presentations of American child. In A. James & A. Prout (Eds.), *Constructing and reconstructing childhood* (pp. 99-117). London: Falmer Press.

Hutton, P.H. (1993). *History as an art of memory*. Hanover, NH: University of New England, University of Vermont.

Hymes, J. (1955). *A child development point of view*. Englewood Cliffs, NJ: Prentice-Hall.

Ingleby, D. (1987). Psychoanalysis and ideology. In J.M. Broughton (Ed.), *Critical theories of psychological development* (pp. 177-210). New York: Plenum Press.

Inhelder, B., & Piaget, J. (1958). *The growth of logical thinking from childhood to adolescence: An essay on the construction of formal operational structures*. New York: Basic Books.

Jipson, J. (1992). The emergent curriculum: Contextualizing a feminist perspective. In S. Kessler & B.B. Swadener (Eds.), *Reconceptualizing the early childhood curriculum* (pp. 149-164). New York: Teachers College Press.

Jolly, H. (1981). *Book of child care: The complete guide of today 's parents*. London: Sphere.

Jones, E. (1953-57). *The life and works of Sigmond Freud*. New York: Basic Books.

Jung, C.G., & Kerenyi, C. (1963). *Essays on a science of mythology: The myth of divine child and the mysteries of Eleusis* (R.C.F. Hull, Trans.). Princeton, NJ: Princeton University Press.

Kagan, J. (1984). *The nature of the child*. New York, NY: Basic Books.

Kagan, J., Kearsley, R., & Zelazo, P. (1978). *Infancy: Its place in human development*. Cambridge, MA: Harvard University Press.

Kagan, S.L., & Garcia, E.E. (1991). Educating culturally and linguistically diverse preschoolers: Moving the agenda. *Early Childhood Research Quarterly, 6*(3), 427-444.

Kamii, C. (1982). *Number in preschool and kindergarten*. Washington, DC: National Association for the Education of Young Children.

Kamii, C. (1985). *Young children reinvent arithmetic: Implications of Piaget's theory*. New York: Teachers College Press.

Kamii, C. (1989). *Young children continue to reinvent arithmetic: Second grade*. New York, NY: Teachers College Press.

Kamii, C. (1993). *Young children continue to reinvent arithmetic: Third grade*. New York: Teachers College Press.

Kamii, C., & DeVries, R. (1978/1993). *Physical knowledge in preschool education: Implications of Piaget's theory*. New York: Teachers College Press.

Kamii, C., & DeVries, R. (1980). *Group games in early education: Implications of Piaget's theory*. Washington, DC: National Association for the Education of Young Children.

Kaplan, P. (1991). *A child's odyssey: Child and adolescent development*. St. Paul, MN: West.

Katz, L. (1996). Child development knowledge and teacher preparation: Confronting assumptions. *Early Childhood Research Quarterly, 11*(2), 145-146.

Kellmer-Pringle, M. (1975). *The needs of children.* London: Hutchinson.

Kelly-Byrne, D. (1989). *A child's play life: An ethnographic study.* New York: Teachers College Press.

Keniston, K. (1976). Psychological development and historical change. In T.K. Rabbs & R.I. Rotberg (Eds.), *The family in history: Interdisciplinary essays* (pp. 75-100). New York: Harper and Row.

Kennedy, D. (1988). Images of the young child in history: Enlightenment and romance. *Early Childhood Research Quarterly, 3,* 121-137.

Kessen, W. (1978). Rousseau's children. *Daedalus, 107* (3), 155-165.

Kessen, W. (1979). The American child and other cultural inventions. *American Psychologist, 34*(10), 815-820.

Kessen, W. (1981). The child and other cultural inventions. In Kessel, F.S., & Siegel, A.W. (Eds.), *The child and other cultural inventions* (pp 26-39). New York: Praeger.

Kessen, W. (1993). A developmentalist's reflections. In G.H. Elder, Jr., J. Model, & R.D. Parke (Eds.), *Children in time and place: Developmental and historical insights* (pp. 226-229). New York: Cambridge University Press.

Kessler, S. (1991). Alternative perspectives on early childhood education. *Early Childhood Research Quarterly, 6* (2), 183-197.

Kessler, S., & Swadener, B.B. (1992). *Reconceptualizing the early childhood curriculum: Beginning the dialogue.* New York: Teachers College Press.

Key, E. (1909). *The century of the child.* New York: G.P. Putnam.

Kincheloe, J. L. (1991). *Teachers as researchers: Qualitative inquiry as a path to empowerment.* New York: Falmer Press.

Kincheloe, J.L. (1993). *Toward a critical politics of teacher thinking.* Westport, CN: Bergin & Garvey.

King, N. (1987). Elementary school play: Theory & research. In J.H. Block & N. King (Eds.), *School play* (pp. 143-166). New York: Garland.

King, N. (1992). The impact of context on the play of young children. In S. Kessler & B.B. Swadener (Eds.), *Reconceptualizing the early childhood curriculum: Beginning the dialogue* (pp. 43-61). New York: Teachers College Press.

King, T., & Fullard, W. (1982). Teenage mothers and their infants: New findings on the home environment. *Journal of Adolescence, 5,* 333-46.

Kitchen, J.M. (1935, March). When babies go to school. *Parent's Magazine, 10,* 16-17.

Klaus, M., & Kennell, J. (1976) *Mother–Infant bonding.* New York: Wiley.

Kliebard, H. (1975). Reappraisal: The Tyler rationale. In W. Pinar (Ed.), *Curriculum theorizing: The reconceptualists* (70-83). Berkeley, CA: McCutchan.

Kliebard, H. (1987). *Struggle for the American curriculum.* London: Routledge and Kegan Paul.

Kohlberg, L. (1976). Moral stages and moralisation. In T. Lickona (Ed.), *Moral development and moral behavior: Theory, research and social issues* (pp. 31-53). New York: Holt, Rinehart & Winston.

Kozol, J. (1991). *Savage inequalities: Children in America's schools.* New York: Harper Perennial.

Laclau, E. (1990). *New reflections on the revolution of our time*. London: Verso.

Lancy, D.F. (1984). Play in anthropological perspective. In P.K. Smith (Ed.), *Play in animals and humans*. Oxford: Basil Blackwell.

Larson, M. (1977). *The rise of professionalism*. Berkeley: University of California Press.

Lasch, C. (1977). *Haven in a heartless world: The family besieged*. New York: Basic Books.

Lather, P. (1991). *Getting smart: Feminist research and pedagogy with/in the postmodern*. New York: Routledge.

Lavine, T. (1984). *From Socrates to Sartre: The philosophic quest*. New York: Bantam Books.

Leach, P. (1988). *Baby and child: From birth to age five*. Harmondsworth: Penguin.

Leavitt, R.L. (1994). *Power and emotion in infant-toddler day care*. Albany: State University of New York Press.

Lerner, G. (1986). *The creation of patriarchy*. New York: Oxford University Press.

Lerner, G. (1993). *The creation of feminist consciousness: From the middle ages to eighteen-seventy*. New York: Oxford University Press.

Lerner, R.M. (1992, Winter). *Diversity*. Newsletter of the Society for Research in Child Development.

Levy, D. (1944). *Maternal overprotection*. New York: Norton.

Lichtman, R. (1987). The illusion of maturation in an age of decline. In J.M. Broughton (Ed.), *Critical theories of psychological development* (pp. 127-148). New York: Plenum Press.

Lillard, P.P. (1996). *Montessori today: A comprehensive approach to education from birth to adulthood.* New York: Schocken books.

Lincoln, Y.S., & Guba, E.G. (1985). *Naturalistic inquiry.* Beverly Hills, CA: Sage.

Lowe, D. (1982). *History of bourgeois perception.* Chicago: University of Chicago Press.

Lubeck, S. (1994). The politics of developmentally appropriate practice. In B. Mallory & R. New (Eds.), *Diversity and developmentally appropriate practices: Challenges for early childhood education.* (pp. 17-39) New York: Teachers College Press.

Lubeck, S. (1996). Deconstructing "child development knowledge" and "teacher preparation." *Early Childhood Research Quarterly, 11*(2), 147-168.

Luke, C. (1989). *Pedagogy, printing, and protestantism: The discourse as childhood.* Albany: State University of New York Press.

Lundberg, F. & Farnham, M. (1947). *Modern women: The lost sex.* New York: Harper.

Lyotard, J. (1984). *The postmodern condition: A report on knowledge,* (G. Bennington and B. Massumi, Trans.). Minneapolis: University of Minnesota Press.

Macedo, D. (1994). *Literacies of power: What Americans are not allowed to know.* Boulder, CO: Westview Press.

Macpherson, C.B. (1962). *The political theory of possessive individualism.* Oxford: Clarendon Press.

Manning, M., & Manning, G. (1989). *Whole language beliefs and practices, K-8.* Washington, DC: National Education Association.

Marshall, H. (1991). The social construction of motherhood: An analysis of childcare and parenting manuals. In A. Phoenix, A. Woollett, & E. Lloyd (Eds.), *Motherhood: Meanings, practices and ideologies.* (pp. 66-85) London: Sage.

Marshall, S. (1991). Childhood in early modern Europe. In J.M. Hawes & N.R. Hiner (Eds.), *Children in historical and comparative perspective* (pp. 53-70). Westport, CT: Greenwood Press.

Martin, J. R. (1986). Redefining the educated person: Rethinking the significance of gender. *Educational Researcher, 15*(6), 6-10.

Matthaei, J. (1982). *An economic history of women in America.* New York: Schocken.

Mattingly, P. (1987). Workplace autonomy and the reforming of teacher education. In T. Popkewitz (Ed.), *Critical studies in teacher education: Its folklore, theory, and practice* (pp. 36-56). New York: Falmer Press.

Mazrui, A. A. (1996). "Progress": Illegitimate child of Judeo-Christian universalism and western ethnocentrism—A third world critique. In L. Marx & B. Mazlish (Ed.), *Progress: Fact or illusion?* (pp. 153-174). An Arbor: The University of Michigan Press.

McCarthy, T. (1991). *Ideals and illusions: On reconstruction and deconstruction in contemporary social theory.* Cambridge: MIT Press.

McDonald, L. & Pien, D. (1982). Mothers conversational behavior as a function of interactional intent. *Journal of Child Language, 8,* 337-58.

McDowell, J.H. (1968). *La nouvelle Heloise. Julie; or, The new Eloise: Letters of two lovers, inhabitants of a small town at the foot of the Alps.* University Park: Pennsylvania State University.

McNally, D. W. (1974). *Piaget, education and teaching.* Sydney: New Educational Press.

Merleau-Ponty, M. (1964). *The primacy of perception.* Evanston, IL: Northwestern University Press.

Miller, D. & Swanson, G. (1958). *The changing American parent.* New York: Wiley.

Mitchell, P. (1992). *The psychology of the child.* London: Falmer.

Mitterauer, M., & Sieder, R. (1982). *The European family.* Chicago: University of Chicago Press.

Montessori, Maria. (1967). *The Montessori method.* (A George, Trans.). Cambridge, MA: Robert Bentley.

Montessori, Mario, Jr. (1976). *Education for human development.* New York: Schocken Books.

Morain, T. (1980). The departure of males from the teaching profession in nineteenth century Iowa. *Civil War History, 27*(2), 161-70.

Morrison, G. S. (1984). *Early childhood education today.* 3rd ed. Columbus, OH: Charles E. Merrill.

Morrow, R.A., with Brown, D.D. (1994). *Critical theory and methodology.* Thousand Oaks, CA: Sage.

Morss, J.R. (1990). *The biologising of childhood: Developmental psychology and the Darwinian myth.* London: Lawrence Erlbaum.

Munro, P. (1996, April). *Catching the "rue " history: Poststructuralism, gender and curriculum history.* American Educational Research Association. New York, NY.

Mussen, P.H. (1970). *Carmichael's manual of child psychology.* New York: Wiley.

NAEYC. (1996). *Guidelines for preparation of early childhood professionals*. Washington, DC: The National Association for the Education of Young Children.

Neill, A.S. (1960). *Summerhill*. New York: Hart.

Nelson, K. (1973). Structure and strategy in learning to talk. *Monographs of the Society for Research in Child Development, 38*:(1-2, No. 149).

New, R. (1990). Excellent early education: A city in Italy has it. *Young Children, 45*(6), 4-10.

Nicholas, D. (1991). Childhood in medieval Europe. In J.M. Hawes, & N.R. Hiner (Eds.), *Children in historical and comparative perspective* (pp. 31-52). Westport, CT: Greenwood Press.

Nicholson, P. (1986). Developing a feminist approach to depression following childbirth. In S. Wilkinson (Ed.), *Feminist social psychology* (pp. 135-150). Milton Keynes: Open University.

Nieuwenhuys, O. (1994). *Children's lifeworlds: Gender, welfare and labour in the developing world*. New York: Routledge.

Noddings, N. (1992) *The challenge to care in schools: An alternative approach to education*. New York: Teachers College Press.

Nsamenang, A.B. (1992). *Human development in cultural context: A third world perspective*. Newbury Park: Sage.

Ochs, E. (1988). *Culture and language socialization in a Samoan village*. Australia: Cambridge University Press.

Ogbu, J.U. (1981). Origins of human competence: A cultural–ecological perspective. *Child Development, 52*, 413-429.

Okin, S.M. (1989). *Justice, gender and the family*. New York: Basic Books.

O'Loughlin, M. (1992, September). *Appropriate for whom? A critique of the culture and class bias underlying developmentally appropriate practice in early childhood education.* Paper presented at the Conference on Reconceptualizing Early Childhood Education: Research, Theory, and Practice, Chicago, IL.

Osborn, D.K. (1991). *Early childhood education in historical perspective.* Athens, GA: Education Associates.

Painter, F.V.N. (1928). *Luther on education.* St. Louis, MO: Concordia Publishing House.

Paley, V. (1979). *White teacher.* Cambridge, MA: Harvard University Press.

Paley, V. (1995). *Kwanzaa and me: A teacher's story.* Cambridge, MA: Harvard University Press.

Parker, F. (1883). *Talks on teaching.* New York: Kellog's Teachers Library.

Parker, F. (1894). *Talks on pedagogies.* New York: E.L. Kellog.

Parten, M. (1932). Social participation among preschool children. *Journal of Abnormal and Social Psychology, 27,* 242-269.

Patterson, C.J. (1992). Children of lesbian and gay parents. *Child Development, 63,* 1025-1042.

Phoenix, A. (1991). Mothers under twenty: Outsider and insider views. In A. Phoenix, A. Woollett, & E. Lloyd (Eds.). *Motherhood: Meanings, practices and ideologies* (pp. 86-102). London: Sage.

Piaget, J. (1957). The child and modern physics. *Scientific American, 197,* 46-51.

Piaget, J. (1964). *The early growth of logic in the child.* New York: Harper.

Piaget, J. (1968). *The psychology of intelligence.* Totowa, NJ: Littlefield, Adams.

Piaget, J. (1970). *Structuralism,* (C. Maschler, Trans.). New York: Harper.

Pinar, W. (1975). Currere: Toward reconceptualization. In W. Pinar (Ed.),*Curriculum theorizing: The reconceptualists* (pp. 396-414). Berkeley: McCutchan.

Pinar, W. (1994). What is reconceptualization? 1978. In *Autobiography, politics and sexuality: Essays in curriculum theory 1972-1992* (pp. 63-74). New York: Peter Lang.

Pinar, W., Reynolds, W., Slattery, P., & Taubman, P. (1995). *Understanding curriculum: An introduction to the study of historical and contemporary curriculum discourses.* New York: Peter Lang.

Pine, J. (1992). Maternal style at the early one-word stage: Re–evaluating the stereotype of the directive mother. *First Language, 12*(Part 2, Number35), 169-86.

Polakow, V. (1982). *The erosion of childhood.* Chicago: The University of Chicago Press.

Popkewitz, T. (1994). Professionalization in teaching and teacher education: Some notes on its history, ideology, and potential. *Teaching and Teacher Education, 10*(1), 1-14.

Popkewitz, T. (1996, April). *The production of reason and power: Curriculum history and intellectual traditions.* Paper presented at the American Educational Research Association, New York, NY.

Poster, M. (1989). *Critical theory and poststructuralism: In search of a context.* Ithaca, NY: Cornell University Press.

Rapp, R. (1987, January). *Reproduction and gender hierarchy: Amniocentesis in contemporary America.* Paper presented at the

International Symposium of the Wenner-Gren Foundation for Anthropological Research. Mijas, Spain.

Reed, G., & Leiderman, P. (1983). Is imprinting an appropriate model for human infant attachment? *International Journal of Behavioral Development, 6*(1), 51–69.

Riley, D. 1983). *War in the nursery: Theories of child and mother.* London: Virago.

Rockhill, K. (1993). Gender, language and the politics of literacy. In B. V. Street (Ed.). *Cross-cultural approaches to literacy* (pp. 156–175). Great Britain: Cambridge University Press.

Rorty, R. (1980). *Philosophy and the mirror of nature.* Oxford: Blackwell.

Rose, N. (1985). *The psychological complex: Psychology, politics and society in England 1869-1939.* London: Routledge & Kegan Paul.

Rose, N. (1990). *Governing the soul: The shaping of the private self.* London: Routledge.

Rosenberg, C.E., & Rosenberg, C.S. (1984). The female animal: Medical and biological views of woman and her role in nineteenth-century America. In J.W. Leavitt (Ed.). *Women and health in America* (pp. 12-27). Madison: University of Wisconsin.

Rousseau, J.J. (1933). *Emile.* (B. Foxley, Trans.). New York: E.P. Dutton.

Rousseau, J.J. (1983). *Emile of over de opvoeding.* Meppel.

Ruch, F. L. (1967). *Psychology and life.* Glenview, IL: Scott Foresman.

Rutter, M. (1981). *Maternal deprivation reassessed.* Harmondsworth: Penguin.

Sawicki, J. (1991). *Disciplining Foucault: Feminism, power, and the body.* New York: Routledge.

Schaffer, H., & Emerson, P. (1964). The development of social attachment in infancy. *Monographs of the Society for Research in Child Development, 29*(3), 1-77.

Schieffelin, B.B. (1990). *The give and take of everyday life: Language socialization of Kaluli children.* New York: Cambridge University Press.

Schwartz, P., & Ogilvy, J. (1979). *The emergent paradigm: Changing patterns of thought and belief* (Analytical Report 7, Values and Lifestyles Program). Menlo Park, CA: SRI International.

Schweinhart, L.J., & Weikart, D.P. (1996). Changed lives, significant benefits: The High/Scope Perry preschool project to date. In K.M. Paciorek & J.H. Munro (Eds.), *Sources: Notable selections in early childhood education* (pp. 337-349). Guilford, CT: Dushkin Publishing Group.

Silin, J.G. (1987). The early childhood educator's knowledge base: A reconsideration. In L. G. Katz (Ed.),*Current topics in early childhood education* (pp. 17-31). Norwood, NJ: Ablex.

Silin, J.G. (1995). *Sex, death, and the education of children: Our passion for ignorance in the age of AIDS.* New York: Teachers College Press.

Singer, E. (1992). *Child care and the psychology of development.* New York: Routledge.

Sklar, K.K. (1973). *Catharine Beecher.* New Haven, CT: Yale University Press.

Skrtic, T.M. (1995). *Disability & democracy: Reconstructing (special) education for postmodernity.* NY: Teachers College Press.

Smith, P.K. (1980). Shared care for young children: alternative models to monotropism. *Merrill Palmer Quarterly, 6*, 371-389.

Solberg, A. (1990). Negotiating childhood: Changing constructions of age for Norwegian children. A. James & A. Prout (Eds.), *Constructing and reconstructing childhood* (pp.118-137). New York: Falmer.

Spencer, H. (1860). *What knowledge is of most worth?* Chapter 1 in *Education*. New York: Appleton.

Spitz, R. (1945). Hospitalism: An inquiry into the genesis of psychiatric conditions in early childhood. *Psychoanalytic Study of the Child, 1*, 53-75.

Spock, B. (1988). *Dr. Spock's baby and child care , 40th Anniversary.* London: Allen.

Steinfels, M. O. (1973). *Who's minding the children? The history and politics of day care in America.* New York: Simon & Schuster.

Stott, F., & Bowman, B. (1996). Child development knowledge: A slippery base for practice. *Early Childhood Research Quarterly, 11*(2), 169-184.

Sullivan, E. (1977). A study of Kohlberg's structural theory of moral development: A critique of liberal social science ideology. *Human Development, 20*, 352-75.

Suttie, I. (1935). *The origins of love and hate.* London: Kegan Paul, Trench, Trubner.

Takanishi, R. (1982). Early childhood education and research: The changing relationship. *Theory into Practice, 20*(2), 86-82.

Taylor-Allen, A. (1982). Spiritual motherhood: German feminists and the kindergarten movement, 1848-1911. *History of Education Quarterly, 22*, 319-339.

Teale, W., & Sulzby, E. (Eds.). (1986). *Emergent literacy: Writing and reading.* Norwood, NJ: Ablex.

Thomas, G., Myer, J., Ramirez, F., & Boli, J. (1987). *Institutional structure: Constituting state, society, and the individual.* Newbury Park, CA: Sage.

Tizard, B. (1991). Employed mothers and the care of young children. In A. Phoenix, A Wollett, & E. Lloyd (Eds.), *Motherhood: Meanings, practices and ideologies* (pp. 178–194). London: Sage.

Tyler, R. (1949). *Basic principles of curriculum and instruction.* Chicago: University of Chicago Press.

United Nations (1959 November 20). Declaration of the rights of the child. In *Resolution 1386 (XIV), Yearbook of the United Nations* (p. 198). New York: United Nations.

Urwin, C. (1985). Constructing motherhood: The persuasion of normal development. In C. Steedman, C. Urwin, & V. Walderdine (Eds.), *Language, gender and childhood* (pp.164-202). London: Routledge.

Vaalsiner, J. (1987). *Culture and the development of children's actions.* Chichester, UK: John Wiley.

van den Berg, J. (1972). *Dubious maternal affection.* Pittsburgh: Duquesne University Press.

Vandewalker, N.C. (1908). *The kindergarten.* New York: Macmillan.

Vann, R. T. (1993). Marxism and historians of the family. In H. Kozicki (Ed.), *Developments in modern historiography* (pp. 139-163). New York: St. Martin's Press.

Viswasnaran, K. (1994). *Fictions of feminist ethnography.* Minneapolis: University of Minnesota Press.

Voneche, J. J. (1987). The difficulty of being a child in French–speaking countries. In J.M. Broughton (Ed.), *Critical theories of psychological development* (pp. 61-86) New York: Plenum Press.

Wadsworth, M. (1986). Evidence from three birth cohort studies for long term and cross–generational effects on the development of children. In M. Richards and P. Light (Eds.), *Children of social worlds* (pp. 116–134). Cambridge: Polity Press.

Waksler, F.C. (1991). Studying children: Phenomenological insights. In F.C. Waksler (Ed.), *Studying the social world of children: Sociological readings* (pp. 60-70). New York: Falmer.

Walkerdine, V. (1984). Developmental psychology and the child-centered pedagogy. In J. Henriques, W. Hollway, C. Urwin, C. Venn, & V. Walkerdine (Eds.), *Changing the subject: Psychology, social regulation and subjectivity* (pp. 153-202). London: Methuen.

Walkerdine, V. (1987). No laughing matter: Girls' comics and the preparation for adolescent sexuality. In J.M. Broughton (Ed.), *Critical theories of psychological development.* (pp. 85–125). London: Plenum Press.

Walkerdine, V. (1988) *The mastery of reason: Cognitive development and the production of rationality.* London: Routledge.

Walkerdine, V. (1990). *Schoolgirl fictions.* London: Verso.

Walderdine, V., & Lucey, H. (1989). *Democracy in the kitchen: Regulating mothers and socialising daughters.* London: Virago.

Walkerdine, V., & the Girls and Mathematics Unit (1989). *Counting girls out.* London: Virago.

Ward, J. (1920) *Psychological principles.* Cambridge: Cambridge University Press.

Weber, E. (1984). *Ideas influencing early childhood education*. New York: Teachers College Press.

Weiner, M. (Ed.). (1966). *Modernization: The dynamics of growth*. New York: Basic Books.

Welter, B. (1979). The cult of true womanhood: 1820-1860. In L. Dinnerstein, & K. Jackson (Ed.) *American Vistas (1607-1877)* (pp. 176–198). New York: Oxford University Press.

White, B.L., Kaban, B.T., & Attanucci, J.S. (1979). *The origins of human competence: The final report of the Harvard preschool project*. Lexington, MA: Lexington Books.

Wolf, F. A. (1981). *Taking the quantum leap*. San Francisco: Harper & Row.

Woodhead, M. (1990). Psychology and the cultural construction of children's needs. In A. James & A. Prout (Eds.), *Constructing and reconstructing childhood* (pp. 60-78). New York: Falmer.

Woollett, A., & Phoenix, A. (1991). Psychological views of mothering. In A. Phoenix, A. Woollett, & E. Lloyd (Eds.), *Motherhood: Meanings, practices, and ideologies* (pp. 28-46). Newbury Park, CA: SAGE.

Wrigley, J. (1991). Different care for different kids: Social class and child care policy. In L. Weis, P.G. Altbach, G.P. Kelly., & H.G. Petrie (Eds.), *Critical perspectives on early childhood education.* (pp. 189-209). Albany: State University of New York Press.

Wylie, P. (1942). *Generation of vipers*. New York: Rinehart.

Zilboorg, G. (1957). The clinical issues of postpartum psychopathological reactions. *American Journal of Obstetric Gynecology, 73*, 305-12.

Author Index

Subject Index

RETHINKING CHILDHOOD

JOE L. KINCHELOE & GAILE CANNELLA, *General Editors*

A revolution is occurring regarding the study of childhood. Traditional notions of child development are under attack, as are the methods by which children are studied. At the same time, the nature of childhood itself is changing as children gain access to information once reserved for adults only. Technological innovations, media, and electronic information have narrowed the distinction between adults and children, forcing educators to rethink the world of schooling in this new context.

This series of textbooks and monographs encourages scholarship in all of these areas, eliciting critical investigations in developmental psychology, early childhood education, multicultural education, and cultural studies of childhood.

Proposals and manuscripts may be sent to the general editors:

Joe L. Kincheloe
c/o Peter Lang Publishing, Inc.
29 Broadway, 18th floor
New York, New York 10006

To order other books in this series, please contact our Customer Service Department at:

(800) 770-LANG (within the U.S.)
(212) 647-7706 (outside the U.S.)
(212) 647-7707 FAX

Or browse online by series at:
www.peterlang.com